Misspeller's
Guide

Misspeller's Guide

Find Correct Spellings Fast
Sort Out Sound-Alikes
Avoid Confusibles

Joel Schroeder
Ruth Schroeder

SkillPath Publications
Mission, Kansas

Project Editor: Kelly Scanlon

Editor: Jane Doyle Guthrie

Cover and Book Design: Rod Hankins

Cover Illustration: Steve Shamburger

Library of Congress Catalog Card Number: 95-72993

ISBN: 1-57294-006-9

10   9   8   7   6   5   4   3   2   1   96   97   98   99   00

Printed in the United States of America

Contents

Introduction

A volunteer received a thank-you letter from a small town mayor, part of which read, "You went above and *beon* the call of duty." The courteousness of the note was all but overshadowed by the magnitude of the spelling errors it contained.

You may have picked up this book because you are a poor speller yourself. Don't feel embarrassed—there may be a number of reasons for your difficulty:

- The English language contains tens of thousands of words, and it's a very fast-growing language too.
- We adopt many foreign words into our language, which carry with them unfamiliar letter combinations and spelling rules.
- You often can spell a sound different ways phonetically (think of all the words that contain the "sh" sound, for example, *tension, fraction,* and *delicious*).
- Spelling rules are sometimes complicated and hard to remember, plus they have many exceptions.

Poor spelling is related to brain function (not intelligence) and the best long-term cure is to work diligently with a good phonics reader such as *Professor Phonics Gives Sound Advice.* But there are some other ways you can combat poor spelling too:

- Use the spell-check function in your word processing software. It's a great tool, plus for most varieties you can add new words to those in the basic memory.
- Develop a working relationship with an up-to-date dictionary. Buy a new one every few years to stay current—and keep it readily accessible.
- Make a check next to every word you look up in the dictionary. If you have to look up a word twice (your check will tell you), put it on your personal misspelled words list.
- Develop tricks to help you remember how to spell difficult words. For example, you want two desserts, so remember to put two S's in *dessert.* Or, the princi*pal* is your pal, and so is money (princi*pal* and interest).

- Use pronunciation to help you visualize correct spellings. That is, overpronounce unusual spellings (such as "Wed-nes-day") and pronounce words precisely (Feb*ru*ary instead of Feb*u*ary).
- When you look up a word in the dictionary, pay attention to spelling clues in the word's origin. For example, the color *fuchsia* was named after a German botanist named *Fuchs*, and *harebrained* means to act like a rabbit.
- Break up a word you have difficulty with into its components and reassemble it:

    mis + spell = misspell

    stubborn + ness = stubbornness
- Write a troublesome word correctly ten times and say it aloud each time. You also learn faster when you involve several senses—see the word, hear it, say it, write it.

Among the thousands of entries included in the "Spelling Guide," you'll find:

- Frequently misspelled common words.
- Frequently misspelled business and professional words (including computer terms).
- Frequently misspelled common foreign words and phrases (such as *adieu* and *cum laude*).
- Frequently misspelled proper nouns like *Cincinnati*.

To use this guide, you can look up a word the way you think it should be spelled (aren't regular dictionaries frustrating for poor spellers?), or you can look up the word the way you think it sounds.

In Part II, "Sound-alikes and Confusibles," you can also check the
meanings of words that either have a similar sound (such as *tide*
and *tied*) or have a similar appearance (such as *persecute* and
prosecute). Words with a potential for misuse because of their
similarities are flagged for you in the "Spelling Guide" so you can
doublecheck anytime you're in doubt.

The sources used to provide the correct spellings offered
here were *Webster's New World Dictionary* (3rd ed.) and *Que's
Computer User's Dictionary* (5th ed.). The words that are
included came from standard lists of words known to give
business writers occasional trouble, but also from people
attending SkillPath seminars. We thank those people for
their help!

Part I

Spelling
Guide

A

WRONG	RIGHT	WRONG	RIGHT
a la kart	a là carte	**abstenshun**	abstention
a la mod	a là mode	**abstrackshun**	abstraction
abaracadabra	abracadabra	**abtrusive**	obtrusive
abayence	abeyance	**abundence**	abundance
abbsens	absence	**abzurd**	absurd
abdicater	abdicator	**acceed**	*accede*
abduck	*abduct*	**accelerater**	accelerator
abducshun	abduction	**acchuary**	actuary
aberant	aberrant	**accidently**	accidentally
aberation	aberration	**accomodate**	accommodate
abestos	asbestos	**accountency**	accountancy
abhorent	abhorrent	**accross**	across
abillity	ability	**acheivement**	achievement
ablueshuns	ablutions	**acknowledgement**	
aboletionist	abolitionist		acknowledgment
abrashun	abrasion	**acolade**	accolade
abreviate	abbreviate	**acolight**	acolyte
absenteism	absenteeism	**acommadate**	accommodate
absess	abscess	**acompaning**	accompanying
absorbshun	*absorption*	**acompany**	accompany
absoreb	*absorb*	**acomplish**	accomplish
absoreption	*absorption*	**acording**	according

WRONG	RIGHT
acost .... accost	**addherent** .... adherent
acountable .... accountable	**addherents** .... *adherents*
acountant ....accountant	**addsorb** .... *adsorb*
acquistion .... acquisition	**addsorption** ....*adsorption*
acquital .... acquittal	**adduck** .... *adduct*
acquited .... acquitted	**adduckshun** .... adduction
acquitence .... acquittance	**addverse** .... *adverse*
acrewal .... accrual	**addvice** ....*advice*
acseed ....*accede*	**ade** .... *aid*
acselerate .... accelerate	**adekwate** .... adequate
acselerater .... accelerator	**adep** .... *adept*
acsentuate .... accentuate	**adew** .... *adieu, ado*
acsept ....*accept*	**adhearants** .... *adherents*
acseptence .... acceptance	**adhearence** .... *adherence*
acsess ....access	**adhearent** .... adherent
acsessable .... accessible	**adhereence** .... *adherence*
acsidentally .... accidentally	**adheshun** .... *adhesion*
acumulate .... accumulate	**adhock** .... ad hoc
acuse .... accuse	**adict** .... addict
acustic .... acoustic	**adij** ....adage
acustom .... accustom	**adinfinitum** .... ad infinitum
acuterment ....accouterment	**adition** .... *addition*
acwaintence ....acquaintance	**adjative** .... adjective
acwess .... acquiesce	**adjur** .... *adjure*
acwire .... acquire	**adjusttment** ....adjustment
ad hok .... ad hoc	**adekwate** .... adequate
ad infenitum .... ad infinitum	**administrater** .... administrator
ad* ....*add*	**admirashun** .... admiration
adalescence ....*adolescence*	**admitence** ....admittance
adalescents .... *adolescents*	**adolesence** ....*adolescence*
adap ....*adapt*	**adolesent** .... adolescent
adaquate .... adequate	**adop** .... *adopt*
Adarondack .... Adirondack	**adreenal** .... adrenal

The asterisk (*) next to boldface words flags "misspellings" that are also real words. For words that appear in italics, see Part II, "Sound-Alikes and Confusibles," to confirm your word choice.

WRONG	RIGHT
adreniline	adrenaline
adress	address
adroytness	adroitness
adsorbent	absorbent
adsorpsion	*adsorption*
adulterater	adulterator
adulteror	adulterer
advantagous	advantageous
adverbeal	adverbial
advertisment	advertisement
advertize	advertise
adveyes	*advise*
advokasy	advocacy
aet	*ate, eight*
aeteen	eighteen
afability	affability
afect	affect
afeild	afield
affadavit	affidavit
affilyate	affiliate
afidavit	affidavit
afinity	affinity
afirm	affirm
afiseonado	aficionado
afix	affix
afixiate	asphyxiate
aflict	afflict
afluence	affluence
afluent	affluent
aford	afford
aforism	aphorism
afrayed	afraid
afrodisiac	aphrodisiac
agast	aghast

WRONG	RIGHT
ageing	aging
aggresion	aggression
aggrivate	aggravate
aginst	against
agonise	agonize
agorafobia	agoraphobia
agrandized	aggrandize
agravate	aggravate
agrecultural	agricultural
agregious	egregious
agressif	aggressive
agression	aggression
agrivate	aggravate
ahoi	ahoy
aile	*ail, ale*
ailmint	ailment
ainjel	*angel*
airalist	aerialist
aireal	aerial
airess	heiress
airloom	heirloom
airomatic	aromatic
ait	*ate, eight*
ajatent	adjutant
ajaysent	adjacent
ajenda	agenda
ajensees	agencies
ajitation	agitation
ajoin	*adjoin*
ajourn	*adjourn*
ajudicating	adjudicating
ajurn	*adjourn*
ajust	adjust
ajustable	adjustable

WRONG	RIGHT	WRONG	RIGHT
akapella	a capella	**alamode**	a là mode
akchewality	actuality	**Alasca**	Alaska
aker	acre	**alay**	*allay*
akilles	Achilles	**Alberkerkee**	Albuquerque
akknowledge	acknowledge	**alcaloid**	alkaloid
akme	*acme*	**alcamist**	alchemist
aknee	*acne*	**alean**	alien
aknowledge	acknowledge	**aledge**	allege
aknowledgement		**aledged**	alleged
	acknowledgment	**aleeus**	alias
akolites	acolytes	**alegation**	allegation
akrid	acrid	**alegiance**	allegiance
akrilic	acrylic	**alement**	ailment
akrimony	acrimony	**alergy**	allergy
akrostic	acrostic	**alerjic**	allergic
aksel	axle	**alewf**	aloof
akselerator	accelerator	**alfa**	alpha
aksent	accent	**algorithem**	algorithm
aksept	*accept*	**aliazing**	aliasing
aksess	*access*	**alies**	*allies*
aksessories	accessories	**aligator**	alligator
aksessory	accessory	**aline**	*align, A-line*
akseum	axiom	**alinement**	alignment
aksis	axis	**aljabra**	algebra
aksunable	actionable	**all most**	almost
akustical	acoustical	**all ways**	*always*
akute	acute	**Allabama**	Alabama
akwaintence	acquaintance	**Allaganey**	Allegheny
akwiesce	acquiesce	**alledge**	allege
akwire	acquire	**alleies**	*alleys*
akwisishun	acquisition	**allerjic**	allergic
alabi	alibi	**alli**	*ally*
alakart	a là carte	**allimentary**	alimentary

The asterisk (*) next to boldface words flags "misspellings" that are also real words. For words that appear in italics, see Part II, "Sound-Alikes and Confusibles," to confirm your word choice.

WRONG	RIGHT	WRONG	RIGHT
allmamator	alma mater	ambasador	ambassador
allot*	*a lot*	ambeant	ambient
allottment	allotment	ambishus	ambitious
alloud	*aloud, allowed*	amblatory	ambulatory
allowence	allowance	ameable	amiable
allredy	*all ready, already*	ameba	amoeba
allthough	although	amenaties	amenities
alltogether	*all together,*	amenaty	amenity
	altogether	amfetamine	amphetamine
alltrueistic	altruistic	amfibian	amphibian
allways	*all ways, always*	ammend	*amend*
alma mayter	alma mater	ammidextrous	ambidextrous
alocate	allocate	amneesha	amnesia
alood	allude	amneosentesis	amniocentesis
alot	*a lot, allot*	amnestee	amnesty
alotment	allotment	amorfus	amorphous
alovera	aloe vera	amortazation	amortization
alowed	*allowed*	amortise	amortize
alredy	*all ready, already*	ampetheater	amphitheater
alright	all right	amwar	armoire
altietude	*altitude*	amyable	amiable
altir	*altar, alter*	Anahime	Anaheim
altrueism	altruism	anakronism	anachronism
altrueistic	altruistic	analagus	analogous
alude	allude	analaseas	analyses
alure	allure	analasis	analysis
alusadation	elucidation	analise	analyze
Alushan	Aleutian	analist	*analyst*
alusion	allusion	analitical	analytical
Alzhimer's	Alzheimer's	analjesic	analgesic
amachur	amateur	anamism	animism
amalgamashun	amalgamation	anamosity	animosity
amallgamate	amalgamate	anarky	anarchy
ambadextrous	ambidextrous	anasteesha	anesthesia

WRONG	RIGHT	WRONG	RIGHT
ancured	anchored	**ansestree**	ancestry
androjanous	androgynous	**ansillary**	ancillary
Andromada	Andromeda	**antagonizm**	antagonism
aneemia	anemia	**antahistameen**	antihistamine
aneemic	anemic	**antartic**	antarctic
anelog	analog or analogue	**antasedent**	antecedent
anestetic	anesthetic	**antaseptic**	antiseptic
anexation	annexation	**antatoxin**	antitoxin
angal	*angle*	**antaydaluvian**	antediluvian
anglasize	Anglicize	**antecipation**	anticipation
angryer	angrier	**anteek**	antique
angshus	anxious	**anteeroom**	anteroom
angsiety	anxiety	**antena**	antenna
anguler	angular	**antequitee**	antiquity
anihilate	annihilate	**antevirus**	antivirus
anjel	*angel*	**anthrapologist**	anthropologist
anjina	angina	**anticedent**	antecedent
ankor	anchor	**antiedote**	*antidote*
Ankoraj	Anchorage	**antikwated**	antiquated
annadote	*anecdote, antidote*	**antisipate**	anticipate
annialate	annihilate	**antisipation**	anticipation
annidote	*antidote*	**antistadic**	antistatic
annoint	anoint	**antonim**	antonym
annoynted	anointed	**antrapology**	anthropology
ano Domini	Anno Domini	**anturash**	entourage
anomlus	anomalous	**anual**	*annual*
anonamus	anonymous	**anuity**	annuity
anorrexia	anorexia	**anul**	*annul*
anounsement	announcement	**anunsiashun**	annunciation
anoy	annoy	**anurism**	aneurysm
anoyed	annoyed	**anvelope**	*envelope*
anser	answer	**anwe**	ennui
ansestor	ancestor	**any one***	*anyone*

The asterisk (*) next to boldface words flags "misspellings" that are also real words. For words that appear in italics, see Part II, "Sound-Alikes and Confusibles," to confirm your word choice.

WRONG	RIGHT	WRONG	RIGHT
anyone*	*any one*	apreshabul	appreciable
apachur	aperture	aprise	*apprise, apprize*
apal	appall	apropo	apropos
apaling	appalling	apropriate	appropriate
aparatus	apparatus	aproximate	*approximate*
aparent	apparent	aquaryum	aquarium
aparition	apparition	araignment	*arraignment*
aparthead	apartheid	aral	*aural*
apastolik	apostolic	aramatic	aromatic
apearance	appearance	arange	orange
apeasement	appeasement	arangement	*arrangement*
apendage	appendage	aranje	*arrange*
apendicks	appendix	arant	*errant*
aperchur	aperture	Arazona	Arizona
apetite	appetite	arbatrary	arbitrary
aplum	aplomb	arbatrate	arbitrate
apocrephal	apocryphal	arbatration	arbitration
apokalips	apocalypse	Arcansaw	Arkansas
apon	upon	arcive	archive
apostrafee	apostrophe	ardueus	arduous
apothacary	apothecary	arears	arrears
apoxy	epoxy	arec	*arc*
app	apt	argile	argyle
apparle	apparel	argueing	arguing
appeerance	appearance	arguement	argument
appendisitis	appendicitis	arie	*airy*
appertif	aperitif	aristacratic	aristocratic
applience	appliance	ark*	*arc*
appresiate	appreciate	arkaic	archaic
appropreate	appropriate	arkane	arcane
apraise	*appraise*	arkatek	architect
aprehend	apprehend	arkatekchure	architecture
aprehension	apprehension	arkeology	archaeology or archeology
aprentise	apprentice		

WRONG	RIGHT	WRONG	RIGHT
arkitecture	architecture	asemmatry	asymmetry
arkive	archive	asender	ascender
Armagedon	Armageddon	asenshun	ascension
armastise	armistice	asent	*ascent, assent*
armer	armor	asert	assert
armstice	armistice	asess	*assess*
aroara	aurora	asessment	assessment
arobics	aerobics	asetasism	asceticism
arodynamic	aerodynamic	asets	assets
arogant	arrogant	asfixiate	asphyxiate
arrable	arable	ashan	ashen
arrain	*arraign*	ashure	assure
arrainment	*arraignment*	asideus	assiduous
arrangment	*arrangement*	asidusly	assiduously
arrouse	arouse	asighlum	asylum
arsinic	arsenic	asimilate	assimilate
artaficial	artificial	asimilated	assimilated
artereosklerosis	*arteriosclerosis*	asist	assist
arteryal	arterial	asistance	*assistance*
arteshan	artesian	asistants	*assistants*
artficial	artificial	asky	ASCII
artheritis	arthritis	askt	asked
artic	arctic	asma	asthma
artical	article	asperagus	asparagus
artifishal	artificial	asprin	aspirin
artikulate	articulate	aspuration	aspiration
artilery	artillery	assalt	assault
arye	awry	assasin	assassin
asailable	assailable	assembel	assemble
asassin	assassin	assenshun	ascension
asault	assault	assetic	ascetic
asay	*assay*	assimalation	assimilation
asemble	assemble	assnine	asinine

The asterisk (*) next to boldface words flags "misspellings" that are also real words. For words that appear in italics, see Part II, "Sound-Alikes and Confusibles," to confirm your word choice.

WRONG	RIGHT	WRONG	RIGHT
astranomical	astronomical	audishun	audition
astrick	asterisk	audyence	audience
astrinjent	astringent	auful	*awful*
astrofizacist	astrophysicist	auht	*aught*
asyncronous	asynchronous	aukzilary	auxiliary
aszay	*assay*	aul	*all, awl*
atache	attaché	ausome	awesome
atachment	attachment	auspisus	auspices
atempted	attempted	austarity	austerity
atendance	*attendance*	austeer	austere
atendants	*attendants*	Australya	Australia
atenshun	attention	authentacate	authenticate
atest	attest	authered	authored
athelete	athlete	authorazation	authorization
atheletic	athletic	authorise	authorize
athoritative	authoritative	automaticly	automatically
atipacal	atypical	autonnomous	autonomous
atitude	*attitude*	autopseed	autopsied
atmosfear	atmosphere	auxilary	auxiliary
atorneys	attorneys	avanew	avenue
atorny	attorney	avaris	avarice
atracshun	attraction	avarishus	avaricious
atractive	attractive	aveashun	aviation
atreum	atrium	avershun	aversion
atribute	attribute	avertion	aversion
atrofy	atrophy	avirse	*averse*
atroshus	atrocious	avirt	*avert*
attashay	attaché	avokation	*avocation*
attornies	attorneys	avoyd	*avoid*
aucshuneer	auctioneer	avoydence	avoidance
audable	audible	aw	awe
audasity	audacity	awarsh	awash
audator	auditor	awate	await
audatorium	auditorium	aweful	*awful*

WRONG	RIGHT	WRONG	RIGHT
awethentic	authentic	backalaret	baccalaureate
awger	*auger, augur*	bael	*bail, bale*
awgur	*augur, auger*	baer	*bare, bear*
awhile*	*a while*	baering	*baring, bearing*
awiegh	*away, aweigh*	baes	*base, bass*
awksilary	auxiliary	baet	*beat, beet*
awnt	*ant, aunt*	baffel	baffle
awspases	auspices	bage	badge
awsteer	austere	bagle	bagel
Awstrailya	Australia	baid	*bade*
awtamatic	automatic	bailif	bailiff
awthentic	authentic	baje	badge
awthor	author	bakterya	bacteria
awtonome	autonomy	balarena	ballerina
awtonomus	autonomous	balay	ballet
awtum	autumn	baleewick	bailiwick
ax*	*acts, axe*	balense	balance
axilary	axillary	ball*	*bawl*
ay	*aye, eye, I*	ballm	balm
ayk	ache	baloney	bologna
ayl	*ail, ale*	baloon	balloon
aynt	*ant, aunt*	Baltamore	Baltimore
ayr	*air, ere, heir*	banboozle	bamboozle
ayt	*ate, eight*	bandwith	bandwidth
azbestus	asbestos	baned	*band, banned*
azma	asthma	banine	benign
azmatic	asthmatic	bankrupcy	bankruptcy
		bankwet	banquet
		bannaster	bannister
		bans*	*banns*
		bar mizvah	bar mitzvah
bachaler	bachelor	baracuda	barracuda
bacis	*basis*	baraj	barrage

B

The asterisk (*) next to boldface words flags "misspellings" that are also real words. For words that appear in italics, see Part II, "Sound-Alikes and Confusibles," to confirm your word choice.

WRONG	RIGHT	WRONG	RIGHT
barametric	barometric	batery	battery
baratone	baritone	battleyon	battalion
baray	beret	baubul	bauble
barbacue	barbecue	bauled	*bald, baud, bawled*
barbituate	barbiturate	bayanet	bayonet
bareable	bearable	bayger	beggar
bareal	burial	Bayroot	Beirut
bareing	*baring, bearing*	baysh	beige
bareum	barium	bayted	*baited, bated*
bargin	bargain	Baytovan	Beethoven
bargining	bargaining	bazar	*bazaar, bizarre*
barin	*baron, barren*	beastial	bestial
barister	barrister	beday	bidet
barnacul	barnacle	bedlem	bedlam
barracade	barricade	bee*	*be*
barrd	*bard, barred*	beech*	*beach*
barrett	barrette	beekon	beacon
barrin	*baron, barren*	Beetoven	Beethoven
barrle	barrel	begar	beggar
baschion	bastion	begile	beguile
basd	*based, baste*	begining	beginning
baseas	*bases*	begruge	begrudge
basecally	basically	begul	beagle
baseis	*basis*	behavyor	behavior
basel	*basal, basil*	behavyoral	behavioral
basicly	basically	behuve	behoove
basilaca	basilica	beir	*beer, bier*
basilli	bacilli	bekeene	bikini
basillus	bacillus	bekweath	bequeath
basinet	bassinet	bel*	*bell, belle*
bast	*based, baste*	belacose	bellicose
basterd	bastard	bele	*bel, bell, belle*
basul	*basal, basil*	beleif	belief
batasite	beta site	beleivable	believable

WRONG	RIGHT	WRONG	RIGHT
beleive	believe	bikuspid	bicuspid
beligerence	belligerence	bild/biled	*billed, build*
belijerent	belligerent	biline	byline
Beljum	Belgium	bilingwal	bilingual
belvadeer	belvedere	bilj	bilge
benadicshun	benediction	billyus	bilious
benafactor	benefactor	bin*	*been*
benaficiary	beneficiary	binokular	binocular
benafishal	beneficial	biografer	biographer
benafit	benefit	biokemical	biochemical
benefishary	beneficiary	biopcy	biopsy
benefitted	benefited	biosfear	biosphere
benevalence	benevolence	birm	*berm*
benifit	benefit	birst	burst
benine	benign	biscit	biscuit
bere	*beer, bier*	biseej	besiege
Berkly	Berkeley	biseps	biceps
berrth	*berth, birth*	bisicle	bicycle
bery	*berry, bury*	bisk	bisque
beseege	besiege	bisket	biscuit
bete	*beat, beet*	bite	byte
beter/betor	*better, bettor*	bius	bias
bi	*buy, by, bye*	bivwack	bivouac
bial	*bail, bale*	biyou	bayou
bianual	*biannual*	biznez	business
bibleographer	bibliographer	bizy	busy
bibleography	bibliography	bizzar	*bazaar, bizarre*
bibliofile	bibliophile	bla	blah
bienial	*biennial*	blasfamus	blasphemous
biest	biased	blatent	blatant
biet	*bite, byte*	bleu	*blew, blue*
bigatry	bigotry	blitzz	blitz
bigotted	bigoted	blizard	blizzard

The asterisk (*) next to boldface words flags "misspellings" that are also real words. For words that appear in italics, see Part II, "Sound-Alikes and Confusibles," to confirm your word choice.

WRONG	RIGHT
bloc*	*block*
bloch	blotch
blok	*bloc, block*
blonnd	*blond, blonde*
bloo	*blew, blue*
blote	bloat
blouz	blouse
blujon	bludgeon
boch	botch
bochalizm	botulism
bodis	bodice
boer	*boar, boor, bore*
bogh	*bough, bow*
boi/boiy	*boy, buoy*
bokay	bouquet
bol	*bole, boll, bowl*
boldder	*bolder, boulder*
boll*	*bole, bowl*
bolona	bologna
bom	bomb
bombadeer	bombardier
bon voyaj	bon voyage
bona fyde	bona fide
bookeeping	bookkeeping
boolabaise	bouillabaisse
boondoggel	boondoggle
boondoks	boondocks
boorshwaze	bourgeoisie
bor	*boar, boor, bore*
bord	*board, bored*
boreder	*boarder, border*
borish	boorish
bornn	*born, borne, bourne*
borsh	borscht

WRONG	RIGHT
Bostin	Boston
boundries	boundaries
boundry	boundary
bounse	bounce
bountaful	bountiful
bournn	*born, borne, bourn*
bouy	*boy, buoy*
bowd	*bode, bowed*
boyant	buoyant
boykot	boycott
boykoted	boycotted
boystrus	boisterous
brach	*broach*
brade	*braid, brayed*
braek	*brake, break*
brainey	brainy
braize	*braise, braze*
brak	*brake, break*
brakets	brackets
brase	*braize, braze*
braselet	bracelet
bratwirst	bratwurst
bravoe	bravo
brawney	brawny
brayzen	brazen
breach*	*breech*
breatheing	breathing
brech	*breach, breech*
bred*	*bread*
breech*	*breach*
breeth	*breathe*
breezey	breezy
breif	brief
brekfest	breakfast

WRONG	RIGHT	WRONG	RIGHT
brest	breast	**bryar**	*briar, brier*
breth	*breath*	**brydal**	*bridal, bridle*
breued	*brewed, brood*	**bryer**	*briar, brier*
brevary	breviary	**bryerwood**	brierwood
brevaty	brevity	**buble**	bubble
brewch	*brooch*	**bucher**	butcher
bricbrack	bric-a-brac	**bucksom**	buxom
bridel	*bridal, bridle*	**Buddism**	Buddhism
brigadeer	brigadier	**budjet**	budget
brij	bridge	**bukle**	*buccal, buckle*
briket	briquette	**bukshle**	bushel
brillience	brilliance	**bulj**	bulge
brillyant	brilliant	**bullatin**	bulletin
brilyance	brilliance	**bullavard**	boulevard
brissle	bristle	**bullit**	bullet
broadkaster	broadcaster	**bulltin**	bulletin
broccli	broccoli	**bulyen/bulyon**	*boullion, bullion*
broch	*broach, brooch*	**bundul**	bundle
brod	*brewed, brood*	**bunt***	*bundt*
brog	brogue	**buoyent**	buoyant
brokitis	bronchitis	**bureaucrasy**	bureaucracy
bronchyal	bronchial	**bured**	*bird, burred*
brontasaurus	brontosaurus	**burglry**	burglary
broos/broose	*brews, bruise*	**burlesk**	burlesque
broot	*bruit, brut, brute*	**buro/burow**	*burro, burrow*
broshur	brochure	**burows**	bureaus
brouse	browse	**burracracy**	bureaucracy
bruizer	bruiser	**burreau**	bureau
bruksizm	bruxism	**burry**	*berry, bury*
brunet	brunette	**burser**	bursar
bruse	*brews, bruise*	**bus***	*buss*
brusk	brusque	**bushul**	bushel
brutallity	brutality	**busness**	business

The asterisk (*) next to boldface words flags "misspellings" that are also real words. For words that appear in italics, see Part II, "Sound-Alikes and Confusibles," to confirm your word choice.

WRONG	RIGHT
bussul	bustle
but*	*butt*
butchor	butcher
buteek	boutique
butiful	beautiful
buton	button
buzerd	buzzard
by*	*buy, bye*
byas	bias
bycuspid	bicuspid
bydirectional	bidirectional
byfocals	bifocals
bynary	binary
byrd	*bird, burred*
byrth	*berth, birth*
byte*	*bight, bite*

C

WRONG	RIGHT
cabanit	cabinet
cabaray	cabaret
cabosh	kibosh
cabul	cable
cach	*catch*
cacooned	cocooned
cadalac	Cadillac
caduseaus	caduceus
cafay	cafe
cafeen	caffeine
cafteria	cafeteria
cajoel	cajole
caki	khaki
calaber	caliber

WRONG	RIGHT
calaborate	collaborate
calabrate	calibrate
calaflower	cauliflower
calapse	collapse
calarey	calorie
calculater	calculator
calidoscope	kaleidoscope
calistenics	calisthenics
calk	caulk
callender	*calendar, calender, colander*
callus*	callous
callvalry	*Calvary, cavalry*
callygraphee	calligraphy
calokweal	colloquial
calossal	colossal
calseum	calcium
calsify	calcify
camaradery	camaraderie
camelyon	chameleon
camfor	camphor
camoflage	camouflage
campain	campaign
camraderie	camaraderie
camul	camel
canairy	canary
cancelled	canceled
cander	candor
candidasy	candidacy
candul	candle
canidate	candidate
caniness	canniness
canon*	*cannon*
canot	cannot

WRONG	RIGHT	WRONG	RIGHT
cansel	cancel	carring	carrying
cansellation	cancellation	carsinojenic	carcinogenic
canser	cancer	carsinoma	carcinoma
Cansus	Kansas	cart blansh	carte blanche
Cantaberry	Canterbury	cartalage	cartilage
cantalope	cantaloupe	cartell	cartel
capallary	capillary	cartrije	cartridge
capasity	capacity	carying	carrying
capchur	capture	Casarean	Caesarean
cappachino	cappuccino	caseeno	casino
caprees	caprice	casette	cassette
capreshus	capricious	casheer	cashier
captansy	captaincy	cassarole	casserole
caraboo	caribou	castagate	castigate
caracature	caricature	casul	castle
caracter	character	catacism	catechism
caracteristic	characteristic	catagorical	categorical
caracterization	characterization	catagorize	categorize
caralary	corollary	catagory	category
Caralina	Carolina	catalitic	catalytic
carbahydrate	carbohydrate	catapillar	caterpillar
carburator	carburetor	categoracal	categorical
cardiavascular	cardiovascular	cathater	catheter
carefull	careful	catilog	catalog or catalogue
cariculum	curriculum	caukus	caucus
carizmatic	charismatic	causeal	*causal*
carless	careless	cauzation	causation
carod	corrode	cavaleer	cavalier
carple tunel	carpal tunnel	caysh	*cache, cash*
carrage	carriage	cayson	caisson
carrat	*carat, caret, carrot*	ceed	*cede, seed*
carreer	career	ceeling	*ceiling, sealing*
Carribean	Caribbean	ceese	*cease, seas, sees, seize*

The asterisk (*) next to boldface words flags "misspellings" that are also real words. For words that appear in italics, see Part II, "Sound-Alikes and Confusibles," to confirm your word choice.

WRONG	RIGHT
celler	*cellar, seller*
cemetary	cemetery
cervex	cervix
cesion	*cession, session*
chaddel	chattel
chaep	*cheap, cheep*
chainge	change
chainged	changed
chaist	*chased, chaste*
chalenge	challenge
chalise	chalice
champain	champagne
champeon	champion
chandeleer	chandelier
changable	changeable
changeing	changing
chansellor	chancellor
chaple	chapel
charatable	charitable
charyot	chariot
chase lounge	chaise lounge
chasened	chastened
chasis	chassis
chassed	*chased, chaste*
chastize	chastise
chattle	chattel
Checoslavakia	Czechoslovakia
cheeta	cheetah
cheez	cheese
cheif	chief
chepe	*cheap, cheep*
chickanery	chicanery
chily	chilly
Chineez	Chinese

WRONG	RIGHT
chinz	chintz
chire	*choir, quire*
choot	*chute, shoot*
choows/chooz	*chews, choose*
chowe	chow
ciak	kayak
cieling	*ceiling, sealing*
cikada	cicada
ciklone	cyclone
cilinder	cylinder
ciln	*kiln*
cinamon	cinnamon
circut	circuit
cireal	*cereal, serial*
cisturn	cistern
citadle	citadel
civalized	civilized
clamy	clammy
clarafacation	clarification
claraty	clarity
clarevoyence	clairvoyance
classafy	classify
clateral	collateral
claus	*Claus, clause, claus*
claustiphobic	claustrophobic
clearence	clearance
cleptomania	kleptomania
clik	*click, clique*
clim	*climb, clime*
clint	client
clintell	clientele
clipbord	clipboard
clishay	cliché
close*	*clothes*

WRONG	RIGHT	WRONG	RIGHT
cloz	*clothes*	colleejate	collegiate
coaglate	coagulate	colnel	colonel
coaless	coalesce	coloquial	colloquial
coalishun	coalition	colosal	colossal
cocain	cocaine	colume	column
cocanut	coconut	comand	*command*
codasil	codicil	combustabil	combustible
codeen	codeine	combustability	combustibility
coegsist	coexist	comemorate	commemorate
coel	*coal, cole, kohl*	comens	*commence, comments*
coema	*coma*	comensurable	commensurable
coerespondents	*corespondents,*	comensurate	commensurate
correspondence, correspondents		coments	*commence, comments*
coersable	coercible	comission	commission
coershun	coercion	comissioner	commissioner
cognashun	*cognation*	comitted	committed
cognezant	cognizant	comittee	committee
cognishun	*cognition*	commershal	commercial
coinside	coincide	comming	coming
coinsidense	coincidence	commital	committal
cojent	cogent	commitee	committee
cojitate	cogitate	commiting	committing
coket	coquette	committment	commitment
coks	coax	commizerate	commiserate
col	*coal, cole, kohl*	comodities	commodities
colateral	collateral	comodity	commodity
coleage	colleague	compack	compact
coledge	*college*	companee	company
colesterol	cholesterol	compareson	comparison
colision	*collision*	comparitive	comparative
colleaque	colleague	compashun	compassion
collectable	collectible	compatable	compatible
collecter	collector	compatreot	compatriot

The asterisk (*) next to boldface words flags "misspellings" that are also real words. For words that appear in italics, see Part II, "Sound-Alikes and Confusibles," to confirm your word choice.

WRONG	RIGHT	WRONG	RIGHT
competative	competitive	condament	condiment
competision	competition	condaminium	condominium
compinsate	compensate	condem	condemn
complacated	complicated	condement	condiment
complament	complement, compliment	condence	condense
		condesend	condescend
complanet	complaint	condesension	condescension
complasensy	complacency	condishun	condition
complie	comply	conduck	conduct
complyant	compliant	conecal	*conical*
compoot	compute	Coneticut	Connecticut
comprabul	comparable	confecshunary	confectionery
comprahended	comprehended	confered	conferred
comprehensability	comprehensibility	conferrence	conference
comprehensable	*comprehensible*	confeshun	confession
comprehensif	*comprehensive*	confidenshaly	confidentially
compresser	compressor	conflikt	conflict
comprest	compressed	confushun	confusion
compromize	compromise	congradulate	congratulate
compulshun	compulsion	congruwent	congruent
compuncshun	compunction	conjenatal	congenital
computor	computer	conjest	congest
comunacate	communicate	conjunktion	conjunction
comunicable	communicable	conker	conquer
comunikay	communiqué	conotation	connotation
comute	commute	conote	connote
comuter	commuter	consceince	*conscience*
conasur	connoisseur	consceintious	conscientious
concensus	consensus	conscous	*conscious*
concievable	conceivable	consede	concede
concieve	conceive	conseev	conceive
concured	concurred	consence	*conscience*
concusions	concussions	consentrate	concentrate
		consentric	concentric

WRONG	RIGHT	WRONG	RIGHT
consequenshal	consequential	conterdictory	contradictory
conseraj	concierge	contigous	*contiguous*
consert	concert	contimplative	contemplative
conserted	concerted	continjensy	contingency
conservetive	conservative	continus	*continuous*
consession	concession	continyews	continues
consheenchus	conscientious	continyou	continue
conshence	*conscience*	continyul	*continual*
conshus	*conscious*	continyus	continuous*
consilatory	conciliatory	contracshal	contractual
consiliate	conciliate	contrapshun	contraption
consise	concise	contraraly	contrarily
consisstent	consistent	contrarey	contrary
consistancy	consistency	contraseptive	contraceptive
consistant	consistent	contredict	contradict
consoladation	consolidation	controled	controlled
consolashun	consolation	controll	control
consorshum	consortium	controvercy	controversy
conspicueus	conspicuous	controvershal	controversial
conspiratoryal	conspiratorial	contushun	contusion
consquently	consequently	convalesent	convalescent
constru	construe	convaless	convalesce
construck	*construct*	convay	convey
consumate	consummate	convayene	conveyance
consumation	consummation	conveenyense	convenience
consumay	consommé	convenence	convenience
contajon	contagion	convertability	convertibility
contajus	*contagious*	convertable	convertible
contempchus	contemptuous	coobacul	*cubical, cubicle*
contemporaneus	contemporaneous	coodoz	kudos
contemtable	contemptible	cooly	coolly
conterdict	contradict	copeist	copyist
		copeous	copious

The asterisk (*) next to boldface words flags "misspellings" that are also real words. For words that appear in italics, see Part II, "Sound-Alikes and Confusibles," to confirm your word choice.

WRONG	RIGHT	WRONG	RIGHT
coperation	cooperation	cotaj	cottage
copiwriter	*copyrighter, copywriter*	coteree	coterie
		coufee	coffee
copyer	copier	counseler	counselor
copyrite	copyright	counsell/counsil	*counsel, council*
copyriter	*copyrighter, copywriter*	counsiller	*counciller, counselor*
		counterfit	counterfeit
copyus	copious	counterfiter	counterfeiter
copywrite	copyright	coup	*coop, coupe*
cor	*cor, core, corps*	courajus	courageous
corador	corridor	courtous	courteous
corajable	corrigible	covanant	covenant
cordroy	corduroy	cowerd/cowerred	*coward, cowered*
corelate	correlate		
coreographer	choreographer	coyl	coil
coreporeal	*corporeal*	cozmetic	cosmetic
corespondence	*correspondence, correspondents*	cozmic	cosmic
		cosy	cozy
corespondent*	correspondent	crackal	crackle
corjal	cordial	cradenshal	credential
coroborate	corroborate	craft*	*kraft*
corolary	corollary	crape	crepe
corp	*cor, core, corps*	craw	crawl
corperation	corporation	creame	*cream, crème*
corprut	coporate	creashun	creation
corpulant	corpulent	createive	creative
correspondant	correspondent	credable	*credible*
correspondense	*correspondence*	credable	*creditable*
corrollary	corollary	credulus	*credulous*
corse	*coarse, course*	creeate	create
corugate	corrugate	creedence	credence
corupt	corrupt	creem	*cream, crème*
corupted	corrupted	crevase	*crevasse, crevice*
costum	*costume*	crewle	*cruel, crewel*

WRONG	RIGHT	WRONG	RIGHT
crewshal	crucial	**curent**	*currant, current*
crik	*crick*	**curiculum**	curriculum
criket	cricket	**curiocity**	curiosity
criple	cripple	**curlacue**	curlicue
criptic	cryptic	**curriculer**	curricular
crissis	crisis	**curser***	*cursor*
cristallize	crystallize	**curtasy**	courtesy
critasism	criticism	**cutacle**	cuticle
criteek	*critique*	**cuzin**	*cousin*
critick	*critic*	**cwantity**	quantity
critisism	criticism	**cyklone**	cyclone
critisize	criticize	**cyncopation**	syncopation
croos	*crews, cruise*		
crul	*crewel, cruel*		
crysis	crisis		
cryterea	criteria		
cryterion	criterion		
cubacul	*cubical, cubicle*	**da Vinchi**	da Vinci
cuboard	cupboard	**dab**	daub
cueb	cube	**daer**	*dear, deer*
cuebic	cubic	**dafadil**	daffodil
cujel	cudgel	**dainjer**	danger
cukumber	cucumber	**daksoont**	dachshund
cul	cull	**dalapadated**	dilapidated
culanary	culinary	**dalima**	dilemma
culchur	culture	**Dalmashan**	Dalmatian
culenary	culinary	**dameanor**	demeanor
culmanate	culminate	**damensha**	dementia
cumkwat	kumquat	**damension**	dimension
curagous	courageous	**damesticate**	domesticate
curansy	currency	**damm**	*dam, damn*
curant	*currant, current*	**damnashun**	damnation
curensy	currency	**damonstration**	demonstration
		damzel	damsel

D

The asterisk (*) next to boldface words flags "misspellings" that are also real words. For words that appear in italics, see Part II, "Sound-Alikes and Confusibles," to confirm your word choice.

WRONG	RIGHT
dandeline	dandelion
dane	deign
danjerus	dangerous
daringdo	derring-do
daseea	dossier
dasill	docile
databasis	databases
datant	détente
Datona	Daytona
dauter	daughter
daverj	diverge
daversafy	diversity
dawarf	dwarf
daybu	debut
dayley	daily
dayre	*dairy*
dayshavu	déja vu
dayta	data
dayz	*days, daze*
dayze	daisy
daz	*days, daze*
dazling	dazzling
deafy	deify
debacal	debacle
debalchery	debauchery
debanair	debonair
debilatate	debilitate
deboch	*debauch*
debree	debris
debuging	debugging
debutant	debutante
decadance	decadence
decafinated	decaffeinated
decaied	decayed

WRONG	RIGHT
decathalon	decathlon
decieve	deceive
decksterity	dexterity
decorashun	decoration
decrepid	decrepit
decsent	*descent*
dedly	deadly
deduckshun	deduction
deductable	deductible
deduse	deduce
deecayed	decayed
deefakto	de facto
deemfasize	de-emphasize
deestroy	destroy
deethronment	dethronement
deevice	*device*
def	deaf
defalt	default
defamashun	defamation
defasit	deficit
defecsion	*defection*
defekation	*defecation*
defence	defense
defendent	defendant
defensable	defensible
deferance	*deference*
defered	deferred
deferenshal	*deferential*
definate	definite
definately	definitely
defishensy	deficiency
deflecter	deflector
deformaty	deformity
defyant	defiant

WRONG	RIGHT
dehidrate	dehydrate
dejenerashun	degeneration
dekalsified	decalcified
dekayed	decayed
dekeraters	decorators
deklarations	declarations
dekopash	découpage
dekorae	decorate
dekorum	decorum
dekstrose	dextrose
delacatessen	delicatessen
delaterious	deleterious
Delawear	Delaware
deleeryus	delirious
delikasy	delicacy
delikatesen	delicatessen
delinkwency	delinquency
delinyate	delineate
deliryum	delirium
delishus	delicious
deliverence	deliverance
delt	dealt
delush	deluge
delushun	delusion
delux	deluxe
demacrat	democrat
demeaner	demeanor
demensha	dementia
demenshun	dimension
deminish	diminish
deminutive	diminutive
demmur	*demur, demure, demurrer*

WRONG	RIGHT
democracyes	democracies
demodulater	demodulator
demografer	demographer
Demoin	Des Moines
demoralise	demoralize
demurer/demurr	*demur, demure, demurrer*
denazen	denizen
dence	*dense, dents*
denigh	deny
denominater	denominator
deparchur	departure
dependance	*dependence*
dependant	dependent
dependants	*dependents*
depleatable	depletable
deplomat	*diplomat*
deplomate	*diplomate*
deplor	deplore
depo	depot
deportasun	deportation
deposator	depositor
deposatory	depository
deposishun	*deposition*
deposit	deposit
depotism	despotism
deppresheashun	depreciation
depravasion	*depravation*
depravation	*deprivation*
deprekate	*deprecate*
depresheate	*depreciate*
deprivastion	*deprivation*
derainjment	derangement

WRONG	RIGHT
derajable	dirigible
deralicshun	dereliction
deralict	derelict
deravation	derivation
derick	derrick
derj	dirge
derrange	derange
derth	dearth
desable	decibel
desalate	desolate
descreshun	discretion
descreshunery	discretionary
descripsion	description
desecate	*desiccate*
deseedent	decedent
deseesed	*deceased*
desegragate	desegregate
desend	descend
desendant	descendant
desender	descender
desent	*decent*
desentralization	decentralization
desentralize	decentralize
desershun	desertion
deside	decide
desimal	decimal
desintegrate	disintegrate
desireable	desirable
desision	decision
desisive	decisive
desolet	*desolate*
despare	despair
despondant	despondent

WRONG	RIGHT
desprate	*desperate*
despratly	desperately
destratushun	destitution
det	debt
detecshun	detection
detenshun	detention
detered	deterred
deterent	deterrent
deth	death
detoksify	detoxify
detor	debtor
detrac	*detract*
detrament	detriment
detramentle	detrimental
dets	debts
detur	detour
deu	*dew, do, due*
deveashun	deviation
deveate	deviate
devel	devil
develipmental	developmental
develope	develop
developement	development
deversification	diversification
deveus	devious
device*	*devise*
devide	divide
devine	divine
devize	*device*
devizor	*devisor*
devyus	devious
dezignate	designate
dezine	design
dezirable	desirable

WRONG	RIGHT	WRONG	RIGHT
dezire	desire	dijatalis	digitalis
di	*die, dye*	dijatize	digitize
diafram	diaphragm	dijest	digest
diaganal	diagonal	dijestable	digestible
dialisis	dialysis	dijestive	digestive
diaphram	diaphragm	dijestshun	digestion
diareea	diarrhea	dijit	digit
diatishan	dietitian	dijital	digital
dibetes	diabetes	dikotomy	dichotomy
dich	ditch	dilajense	diligence
dictashun	dictation	dilajent	diligent
dictionaryes	dictionaries	dilashun	dilation
dictionery	dictionary	dilema	dilemma
die*	*dye*	dilimma	dilemma
diegress	digress	dilog	dialog or dialogue
dieing	*dying, dyeing*	dimond	diamond
dievers	*divers, diverse*	dinamite	dynamite
difacult	difficult	dinamo	dynamo
difadense	*diffidence*	dinasors	dinosaurs
diference	*difference*	dinasty	dynasty
diferensheate	differentiate	dineing	dining
diferential	*differential*	dinet	dinette
diffrent	different	dingee	*dinghy, dingy*
difidence	*diffidence*	dinjee	*dingy*
difuse	diffuse	dinnor	*dinner*
difushun	diffusion	dinor	*diner*
digestable	digestible	dioseas	diocese
dignafied	dignified	diphragm	diaphragm
dignafy	dignify	dippswitch	DIP switch
dignosis	diagnosis	dipstik	dipstick
digres	digress	diptheria	diphtheria
diing	*dyeing, dying*	dipthong	diphthong
dijatal	digital	direa	diarrhea

The asterisk (*) next to boldface words flags "misspellings" that are also real words. For words that appear in italics, see Part II, "Sound-Alikes and Confusibles," to confirm your word choice.

WRONG	RIGHT
direcshunal	directional
directry	directory
dirijable	dirigible
diry	*diary*
disalusion	*dissolution*
disapate	dissipate
disapear	disappear
disapline	discipline
disapoint	disappoint
disappearence	disappearance
disaprov	*disapprove*
disasemble	*disassemble*
disasociate	disassociate
disastrus	disastrous
disatified	dissatisfied
disbirse	*disburse*
disc*	*disk*
discdrive	disk drive
discharj	discharge
disclamer	disclaimer
discommfert	*discomfort*
discommfit	*discomfit*
disconsert	disconcert
discreat	*discreet, discrete*
discribe	descrie
discus*	*discuss*
dise	dice
diseas	disease
disect	dissect
disection	dissection
diseesed	*diseased*
disemble	*dissemble*
disent	*descent, dissent*
disentary	dysentery

WRONG	RIGHT
disfunctional	dysfunctional
disgise/disgize	disguise
disidence	*dissidence*
disidents	*dissidents*
disilusion	*disillusion*
disimiler	dissimilar
disintersted	disinterested
disipate	dissipate
disipline	discipline
disklosure	disclosure
diskribe	describe
diskrimination	discrimination
diskus	*discus*
disociate	dissociate
disolut	*dissolute*
disolve	dissolve
disonor	dishonor
dispicable	despicable
dispirse	*disperse*
dispozal	disposal
dispozishun	*disposition*
disproporshunate	disproportionate
disprov	*disprove*
dispurse	*disperse*
dissern	discern
dissernable	discernible
dissidant	dissident
dissiminate	disseminate
dissparate	*disparate*
distengwish	distinguish
distingwished	distinguished
distorshun	distortion
distrac	*distract*

WRONG	RIGHT	WRONG	RIGHT
distroy	destroy	doormouse	dormouse
disturbence	disturbance	doplisity	duplicity
divergance	divergence	dormatories	dormitories
divershun	diversion	dormatory	dormitory
divisable	divisible	dorsel	dorsal
diviser	*divisor*	dos	*dose, doze*
divulgance	divulgence	dosyay	dossier
dizastrous	disastrous	dot matrex	dot matrix
diziness	dizziness	dounturn	downturn
dizmal	dismal	dout	doubt
docktrin	doctrine	doutingly	doubtingly
docktrinair	doctrinaire	doutless	doubtless
docsology	doxology	downlode	download
doe*	*dough*	doz	*dose, doze*
doemestic	domestic	drall	drawl
does'nt	doesn't	drapry	drapery
doge	dodge	drege	dredge
dogh	*doe, dough*	drivle	drivel
dokument	document	dromadary	dromedary
dokumentashun	documentation	drout	drought
doly	duly	drugist	druggist
domacile	domicile	dubius	dubious
domanant	dominant	duble	double
domane	domain	dubyus	dubious
domaneer	domineer	duc	*duck*
domestacate	domesticate	duch	dutch
dominent	dominant	ductal	ductile
don	*done, dun*	dueplex	duplex
Don Keowtee	Don Quixote	duked	*ducked, duct*
donashun	donation	dum	dumb
doner	donor	dumbell	dumbbell
doo	*do, dew, due*	dun*	*done, dun*
dooly	duly	dunage	*dunnage*

The asterisk (*) next to boldface words flags "misspellings" that are also real words. For words that appear in italics, see Part II, "Sound-Alikes and Confusibles," to confirm your word choice.

WRONG	RIGHT
dunjon	dungeon
dunn	*done, dun*
duplacate	duplicate
durring	during
duse	deuce
dush	douche
dutaful	dutiful
duv	dove
duzen	dozen
duzen't	doesn't
dy	*die, dye*
dyscomfit	*discomfit*
dyscomfort	*discomfort*
dyscrete	*discreet, discrete*

E

WRONG	RIGHT
ealusive	*elusive*
easle	easel
easyer	easier
easyest	easiest
easyly	easily
eavsdrop	eavesdrop
eaziness	easiness
ecanomical	economical
ech	etch
eclare	eclair
ecleesiastical	ecclesiastical
economacal	economical
ecsentric	eccentric
ectasy	ecstasy
edable	edible
edafication	edification

WRONG	RIGHT
edafy	edify
edator	editor
eddition	*edition*
edeema	edema
Edipus	Oedipus
editting	editing
edukable	*educable*
edusable	*educible*
eeger	eager
eerie*	*aerie*
efacashus	efficacious
efeminate	effeminate
effacasy	efficacy
effervesent	effervescent
efficasy	efficacy
efficeint	efficient
effisency	efficiency
eflewent	*effluent*
eger	eager
Egipt	Egypt
egle	eagle
egosentric	egocentric
egotistacal	egotistical
ehter	*either*
eigteen	eighteen
eigth	eighth
eigtieth	eightieth
ej	edge
Ejip	Egypt
Ejipshun	Egyptian
ejucable	*educable*
ejus	aegis
eklips	eclipse
eko	echo

WRONG	RIGHT
eksaserbate	exacerbate
eksasperashun	exasperation
eksemplary	exemplary
eksemplify	exemplify
eksentric	eccentric
eksershun	exertion
ekskwisite	exquisite
eksonerate	exonerate
eksort	exhort
ekspeediancy	expediency
eksplicable	explicable
ekstasy	ecstacy
ekstenuating	extenuating
ekstink	extinct
ekstort	extort
ekstraneous	extraneous
ekswisite	exquisite
ekwalateral	equilateral
ekwalize	equalize
ekwanoks	equinox
ekwator	equator
ekwitable	*equitable*
ekwivalent	equivalent
elafant	elephant
elajable	*eligible*
elamentary	*elementary*
elastisity	elasticity
electramagnetic	electromagnetic
electrisian	electrician
electrolasis	electrolysis
elegent	elegant
elickir	elixir
eligability	eligibility

WRONG	RIGHT
elijable	*eligible*
elikser	elixir
elimnate	eliminate
elipsis	ellipsis
eliptacal	elliptical
ellevator	elevator
ellicit	*elicit, illicit*
elokwense	eloquence
elonggate	elongate
elusadate	elucidate
email	e-mail
emajinary	imaginary
emanent	*eminent, imminent*
emassary	emissary
embalance	imbalance
embarass	embarrass
embezzel	embezzle
embibe	imbibe
embreo	embryo
embroydry	embroidery
emergancy	emergency
emerj	*emerge*
emfasize	*emphasize*
eminant	eminent
eminashun	emanation
emision	*emission*
emmense	immense
emmploy	employ
emmunity	immunity
empathise	*empathize*
emphasema	emphysema
employes	employees
emty	empty

The asterisk (*) next to boldface words flags "misspellings" that are also real words. For words that appear in italics, see Part II, "Sound-Alikes and Confusibles," to confirm your word choice.

WRONG	RIGHT
emulshun	emulsion
encredible	*incredible*
encripshun	encryption
encrochment	encroachment
encurage	encourage
endojenous	*endogenous*
endorfin	endorphin
endurence	endurance
enerjee	*energy*
enerjetic	energetic
enert	inert
enfest	*infest*
enforcable	enforceable
enfraction	*infraction*
enhanse	enhance
enjeanuous	*ingenuous*
enmass	en masse
enocents	*innocence, innocents*
enoomerat	enumerate
enormaty	enormity
enormus	*enormous*
enosence	*innocence, innocents*
ensacklopedia	encyclopedia
ensembel	ensemble
enshur	*ensure, insure*
ensignificant	insignificant
ensin	ensign
enskans	ensconce
enstants	*instance, instants*
entamology	*entomology*
entegrate	integrate
entegrated	integrated
entents	*intense, intents*
enter*	*inter*

WRONG	RIGHT
entercede	intercede
enterface	interface
enterfere	interfere
enterjection	interjection
enterloper	interloper
enterprize	enterprise
enterrupt	*interrupt*
entersepted	intercepted
enterstate	*interstate*
entervention	intervention
enterview	interview
enterwoven	interwoven
enthusasm	enthusiasm
entraprenur	entrepreneur
entrastate	*intrastate*
entroduce	introduce
enturash	entourage
envade	*invade*
envalope	envelope
envellop	*envelop, envelope*
enventoried	inventoried
envirmentalist	environmentalist
envirnment	environment
envyable	enviable
epademic	*epidemic*
epagram	*epigram*
epagraph	*epigraph*
epalepsy	epilepsy
epasodic	episodic
epatath	*epitaph*
epatheth	*epithet*
epik	*epic*
epitamy	epitome
epitamize	epitomize

WRONG	RIGHT
epock	*epic, epoch*
epokse	epoxy
equiped	equipped
equivalance	equivalence
eqwable	*equable*
eqwitable	*equitable*
eradacable	eradicable
eradacate	eradicate
eraseable	*erasable*
erashur	*erasure*
eraysir	*eraser*
erbal	herbal
erbivore	herbivore
erecshun	erection
erend	*errand*
erent	*errant*
ergonamics	ergonomics
erie	*eerie, Erie*
ern	*earn, erne, urn*
ernnest	*earnest, Ernest*
eroneous	erroneous
eroshun	erosion
erroneus	erroneous
errupt	*erupt*
esay	*essay*
eschuary	estuary
escro	escrow
esence	essence
eshalan	echelon
eskalashun	escalation
Eskamo	Eskimo
eskorted	escorted
esofagus	esophagus

WRONG	RIGHT
espeshally	especially
espianaj	espionage
espree de kor	esprit de corps
establishmint	establishment
estemate	estimate
estemed	esteemed
esthetic	aesthetic or esthetic
eteemology	etymology
eteology	*etiology*
eternel	eternal
ethacal	ethical
ethicks	*ethics*
ethil	ethyl
ethnicks	*ethnics*
ettiquette	etiquette
eue	*ewe, yew, you*
evadenshal	evidential
evadent	evident
evakuate	evacuate
evaluetion	evaluation
evalushun	evolution
evanjalize	evangelize
evanjelacal	evangelical
evenchual	eventual
eventfull	eventful
everyday*	*every day*
everyone*	*every one*
evicshun	eviction
evidenshary	evidentiary
evin	even
evinsible	evincible
evolushun	evolution
exabishun	exhibition

The asterisk (*) next to boldface words flags "misspellings" that are also real words. For words that appear in italics, see Part II, "Sound-Alikes and Confusibles," to confirm your word choice.

WRONG	RIGHT
exagerate	exaggerate
exaserbate	exacerbate
excede	*exceed*
excellant	excellent
exceptible	acceptable
exceptionaly	exceptionally
excesive	excessive
excutive	executive
executer	executor
exemplafy	exemplify
exersize	exercise
exhaustable	exhaustible
exhibtion	exhibition
exilerate	exhilarate
existance	existence
exkuse	excuse
exorbatent	exorbitant
exortation	exhortation
expance	expanse
expearence	experience
expeate	expiate
expediate	expedient
expedishus	expeditious
expedyence	expedience
expence	expense
expendible	expendable
experament	experiment
experiance	experience
explaination	explanation
expoenshal	exponential
expoensheation	exponentiation
expresive	expressive
exquisit	exquisite
exsel	excel

WRONG	RIGHT
exsellent	excellent
exsept	except
exseptionally	exceptionally
exsessive	excessive
exsize	excise
exspreso	espresso
extemporanous	extemporaneous
extenshun	extension
exterdite	extradite
exterordinaire	extraordinaire
exterordinary	extraordinary
extradishun	extradition
extravagence	extravagance
extreemly	extremely
extrordinary	extraordinary
exuberent	exuberant
exume	exhume
eyeglases	eyeglasses
eyesometric	isometric
eying	eyeing

F

WRONG	RIGHT
fabracate	fabricate
fabulus	fabulous
fachul	factual
facshun	faction
faet	*fate, fete*
faet	*feat, feet*
fain*	*feign*
Fairenhite	Fahrenheit
fakshus	*factious*

WRONG	RIGHT	WRONG	RIGHT
faksimalee	facsimile	**fashal**	facial
fakulty	faculty	**fashism**	fascism
faiz	*faze, phase*	**fashon**	fashion
fallable	fallible	**fasidious**	fastidious
fallasy	fallacy	**fasil**	facile
falonyus	felonious	**fasilitate**	facilitate
falopian	fallopian	**fasilities**	facilities
falt	fault	**fasility**	facility
falty	faulty	**fasinate**	fascinate
famaldehyde	formaldehyde	**fasinating**	fascinating
familure	familiar	**fasination**	fascination
famus	famous	**fastner**	fastener
fanatasism	fanaticism	**fatail**	fatal
fane	*fain, feign*	**fathum**	fathom
fanetic	phonetic	**fatig**	fatigue
fantesy	fantasy	**fauset**	*faucet*
fantom	phantom	**favortism**	favoritism
Farenhite	Fahrenheit	**fawn***	*faun*
farey	*fairy, ferry*	**fayker**	*faker, fakir*
fariner	foreigner	**faynt**	*faint, feint*
farmasist	pharmacist	**feancay**	*fiance, fiancee*
farmasudical	pharmaceutical	**feasable**	feasible
farmasy	pharmacy	**feasco**	fiasco
faroshus	ferocious	**Febuary**	February
farre	*fair, fare*	**fech**	fetch
farsical	farcical	**federasion**	federation
farthir	*farther*	**feebul**	feeble
fary	*fairy, ferry*	**feechur**	feature
fasade	facade	**feeld**	field
fase	face	**feers**	fierce
faseel	facile	**feest**	feast
faseshus	*facetious*	**feet***	*feat*
faset	*facet*	**feetal**	fetal

The asterisk (*) next to boldface words flags "misspellings" that are also real words. For words that appear in italics, see Part II, "Sound-Alikes and Confusibles," to confirm your word choice.

WRONG	RIGHT	WRONG	RIGHT
fein	*fain, feign*	figet	fidget
feind	fiend	figyer	figure
feirce	fierce	fiktishus	*fictitious*
felisity	felicity	filabuster	filibuster
feloneous	felonious	Filadelphia	Philadelphia
femilyer	familiar	filaktery	phylactery
fenomenal	phenomenal	filander	philander
fenomenon	phenomenon	filanthropy	philanthropy
feret	ferret	Filapeens	Philippines
feroshus	ferocious	filharmonic	philharmonic
fers	*firs, furs, furze*	fillter	*filter, philter*
ferst	first	filosofer	philosopher
fertalizer	fertilizer	filosofy	philosophy
fertle	fertile	finaly	*finale, finally, finely*
fervant	fervent	finanseer	financier
ferver	*fervor*	finanshal	financial
fery	*fury*	finnagle	finagle
fesability	feasibility	finned	*find, fined*
fesable	feasible	finnes	finesse
fesant	pheasant	finry	finery
festaval	festival	firlo	furlough
festivatees	festivities	firlongs	furlongs
fete*	*feat, feet*	firment	*ferment*
fether	feather	firy	fiery
fettid	fetid	fisacal	*physical*
fewd	feud	fisacally	physically
fewdal	feudal	fiseek	*physique*
fewtile	futile	fishor	*fisher, fissure*
fiar	*fair, fare*	fisishan	physician
fibrus	fibrous	fiskal	*fiscal*
fictishus	*fictitious*	fisty	feisty
fidusheary	fiduciary	fistycufs	fisticuffs
fieting	fighting	fisure	*fisher, fissure*
fiftith	fiftieth	fite	fight

WRONG	RIGHT	WRONG	RIGHT
fiz	*fizz, phiz*	flor	*flour, flower*
fizeolojacal	physiological	Florada	Florida
fizics	physics	floradation	fluoridation
flabergast	flabbergast	floressent	fluorescent
flagalate	flagellate	floride	fluoride
flagrent	*flagrant*	floter	floater
flak*	*flack*	flount	*flaunt*
flamable	flammable	flouwer	*flour, flower*
flamboyence	flamboyence	flowt	*flout*
flannle	flannel	fluchewashun	fluctuation
flare*	*flair*	flucks	flux
flasid	flaccid	flue*	*flew, flu*
flawnt	*flaunt*	flurish	flourish
flayr	*flair, flare*	flywait	flyweight
fle	*flea, flee*	fo	foe
flecs	*flecks, flex*	foament	*foment*
fleese	fleece	fobia	phobia
fleez	*fleas, flees*	foder	fodder
flegling	fledgling	foepa	faux pas (sing. and plur.)
flem	phlegm	foerward	*foreword, forward*
flewent	fluent	fogey	*foggy, fogy*
flexability	flexibility	fok	folk
flexable	flexible	folacle	follicle
flexs	*flecks, flex*	folaj	foliage
flier	flyer	fole	foal
flirtashun	flirtation	foleashun	foliation
flite	flight	foled	*foaled, fold*
flo	*floe, flow*	follacal	follicle
flok	*floc, flock*	fome	foam
floo	*flew, flu, flue*	fonddling	*fondling*
floorist	florist	fone	phone
floppie disc	floppy disk	fonetic	phonetic
floppyes	floppies	fonograph	phonograph

The asterisk (*) next to boldface words flags "misspellings" that are also real words. For words that appear in italics, see Part II, "Sound-Alikes and Confusibles," to confirm your word choice.

WRONG	RIGHT	WRONG	RIGHT
fony	phony	fornacation	fornication
foo	few	fors	force
foochur	future	forsee	foresee
foomagate	fumigate	forseps	forceps
foor	*for, fore, four*	forsible	forcible
foosalaj	fuselage	fort*	*forte*
for*	*fore, four*	fortafacation	fortification
forarm	forearm	fortay	*forte*
forbad	forbade	forteen	fourteen
forbare	*forbear, forebear*	forth*	*fourth*
forbareence	forbearance	fortith	fortieth
forcable	forcible	fortuatus	fortuitous
forchunate	fortunate	forword	*foreword, forward*
forchunately	fortunately	fosfurus	phosphorous
forclose	foreclose	fosil	fossil
forcloshur	foreclosure	foter	footer
forebare	*forbear, forebear*	fotoelectic	photoelectric
foregn	foreign	fotograph	photograph
forelorn	forlorn	fotographic	photographic
foremally	*formally*	fotojenic	photogenic
foresithia	forsythia	fotosinthesis	photosynthesis
foreswear	forswear	fotostat	photostat
foreth	*forth, fourth*	fotostatic	photostatic
foreward	*foreword, forward*	foul*	*fowl*
forfit	forfeit	foundasion	foundation
forgoten	forgotten	fountin	fountain
forhead	forehead	fourbear	*forbear, forebear*
forin	foreign	fourty	forty
formadable	formidable	fourword	*foreword, forward*
formaly	*formally*	fout	fought
formating	formatting	fowndling	*foundling*
formdable	formidable	fragrence	fragrance
formmerly	*formerly*	fragrent	*fragrant*
formoola	formula	frajewlent	fraudulent

WRONG	RIGHT
frajil	fragile
franc*	*frank*
franchize	franchise
frantick	*frantic*
frase	*frays, phrase*
fraternaty	fraternity
fraternel	fraternal
frayt	freight
fraze	*frays, phrase*
frazel	frazzle
frazology	phraseology
freese	*freeze, frieze*
freeze*	*frieze*
freind	friend
freize	*freeze, frieze*
frekle	freckle
frekwency	frequency
frekwent	frequent
frendly	friendly
frentic	*frenetic*
freqwent	frequent
freqwently	frequently
frier	*friar, fryer*
frijid	frigid
frikshun	friction
frinj	fringe
frivalus	frivolous
frizul	frizzle
Froid	Freud
frolicing	frolicking
froot	fruit
fruishun	fruition
fruitose	fructose

WRONG	RIGHT
fryar	*friar, fryer*
fuchur	future
fuge	fudge
fujative	fugitive
fuled	furled
fullfil	fulfill
fumagate	fumigate
funareal	*funereal*
fundimental	fundamental
funel	funnel
funkshun	function
funneral	*funeral*
funnle	funnel
furnature	furniture
furrey	*furry*
furrs	*firs, furs, furze*
furthir	*further*
fusalage	fuselage
fusha	fuchsia
fyle	*faille, file*
fysty	feisty

G

WRONG	RIGHT
gaberdeen	gabardine
gaet	*gait, gate*
gaf/gafe	*gaff, gaffe*
gage*	*gauge*
galarea	galleria
galashes	galoshes
galavant	gallivant
gallent	gallant

The asterisk (*) next to boldface words flags "misspellings" that are also real words. For words that appear in italics, see Part II, "Sound-Alikes and Confusibles," to confirm your word choice.

WRONG	RIGHT	WRONG	RIGHT
gallz	gauze	ginacological	gynecological
gambel	*gamble*	ginacology	gynecology
gambowl	*gambol*	girnee	gurney
gangreen	gangrene	gitar	guitar
garantee	*guarantee*	gize	*guise, guys*
garanty	*guaranty*	gizer	geyser
garason	garrison	glamerus	glamorous
gard	guard	glammer	glamour
gardean	guardian	glashal	glacial
gargoil	gargoyle	glayshur	*glacier*
gargul	gargle	glayzer	*glazier*
garilla	*gorilla, guerrilla*	glisens	glistens
garneshmet	garnishment	gliserin	glycerin
gasaleen	gasoline	glooey	*gluey*
gastly	ghastly	gluttonus	gluttonous
gauntlet*	*gantlet*	goey	*gooey*
gayaty	gaiety	goldin	golden
gayge	*gage, gauge*	gontlet	*gantlet, gauntlet*
gayt	*gait, gate*	goobanatorial	gubernatorial
geans	*genes, jeans*	good will	goodwill
geloshs	*galoshes*	goofey	goofy
gendre	genre	gool	ghoul
geneology	genealogy	gord	*gourd, gourde*
genuiness	genuineness	Gorja	Georgia
gerrila	*gorilla, guerrilla*	gormand	*gourmand*
gess	guess	gormay	*gourmet*
gest	*guessed, guest*	gorrila	*gorilla, guerrilla*
getto	ghetto	gosamer	gossamer
gib	*gibe, jibe*	gost	ghost
gide	*guide, guyed*	govenor	governor
gile	guile	goverened	governed
gilld	*gild, guild*	goverment	government
gillt	*gilt, guilt*	govnor	governor
gimick	gimmick	gra	gray

WRONG	RIGHT	WRONG	RIGHT
graaft	*graft, graphed*	**greevence**	grievance
gradyent	gradient	**gregarius**	gregarious
graet	*grate, great*	**greivance**	grievance
graf	*graph*	**greivous**	grievous
grafeete	graffiti	**grevance**	grievance
grafic	graphic	**grevous**	grievous
grafite	graphite	**gridle**	griddle
graider	*grader*	**gril**	*grill, grille*
grait	*grate, great*	**gripp**	*grip, grippe*
graiter	*grater, greater*	**grissly**	*grisly*
grajul	gradual	**gristlee**	*gristly*
grammatacal	grammatical	**grizly**	*grizzly*
grammer	grammar	**groll**	growl
grandeoss	grandiose	**gron**	*groan, grown*
grandur	grandeur	**grotesk**	grotesque
granit	*granite*	**groth**	growth
granuler	granular	**gruge**	grudge
grase	grace	**grugingly**	grudgingly
grashus	gracious	**grup**	group
gratafy	gratify	**grusum**	gruesome
grate*	*great*	**grype**	*gripe*
gratful	grateful	**guantity**	quantity
gratuatus	gratuitous	**guelt**	*gilt, guilt*
gratuaty	gratuity	**guidence**	guidance
gravatate	gravitate	**guilotine**	guillotine
gravle	gravel	**guiter**	*quitter*
grayter	*grater, greater*	**gulash**	*goulash*
grayz	*grays, graze*	**guld**	*gild, guild*
greatful	grateful	**gullability**	gullibility
greef	grief	**gullable**	gullible
Greesan	Grecian	**guned**	gunned
greese	*grease, Greece*	**gurgel**	gurgle
greev	grieve	**gurnee**	gurney

The asterisk (*) next to boldface words flags "misspellings" that are also real words. For words that appear in italics, see Part II, "Sound-Alikes and Confusibles," to confirm your word choice.

WRONG	RIGHT	WRONG	RIGHT
gurrilla	*gorilla, guerrilla*	**harlaquin**	harlequin
gussler	guzzler	**harpsacord**	harpsichord
guvanor	governor	**harrass**	harass
guyser	geyser	**hart***	*heart*
gys	*guise, guys*	**harty**	hearty
		hastile	*hostile*

H

WRONG	RIGHT	WRONG	RIGHT
		haszel	hassle
		hatefull	hateful
habatat	habitat	**hav**	*halve, have*
habichual	habitual	**haw***	*hall, haul*
hai	*hay, hey*	**Hawhyee**	Hawaii
haif	*halve*	**hawty**	haughty
hail*	*hale*	**hay***	hey
hair*	*hare*	**hayr**	*heir*
hairasy	*heresy*	**hazzard**	hazard
hairbrained	harebrained	**headress**	headdress
hakneed	hackneyed	**hebache**	hibachi
halarious	hilarious	**hedache**	headache
hale*	*hail*	**hedder**	header
hall*	*haul*	**heer**	*hear, here*
halocost	holocaust	**heet**	heat
haloosanate	hallucinate	**hege**	hedge
halusinojen	hallucinogen	**hei**	*hi, hie, high*
hamer	hammer	**heid**	*hide, hied*
handework	handiwork	**heil**	*heal, heel*
handul	handle	**helacopter**	helicopter
hanger*	*hangar*	**hele**	*heal, heel*
hankerchief	handkerchief	**helmit**	helmet
haphazzard	haphazard	**helth**	health
harang	harangue	**helthy**	*healthy*
harber	harbor	**hemaroids**	hemorrhoids
harbinjer	harbinger	**hemisfere**	hemisphere
hardin	harden	**hemofilia**	hemophilia
hare*	*hair*	**hemofiliac**	hemophiliac

WRONG	RIGHT
hemorage	hemorrhage
hemorroid	hemorrhoid
Hendu	Hindu
heras	harass
herasy	*heresy*
herawin	*heroin, heroine*
herbaside	herbicide
herd*	*heard*
here*	*hear*
heredatary	hereditary
heresay	*hearsay*
heretage	heritage
hermatage	hermitage
heros	heroes
herowin	*heroin, heroine*
hesatent	hesitant
hetrojeaneus	heterogeneous
heu	*hew, hue*
heven	heaven
hevier	heavier
hevy	heavy
hew*	*hue*
hi*	*hie, high*
hiar	*higher, hire*
hiarchy	hierarchy
hibranate	hibernate
hibrid	hybrid
hich	hitch
hideus	hideous
hidralic	hydraulic
hidrant	hydrant
hidrawlic	hydraulic
hidrojin	hydrogen

WRONG	RIGHT
hidrokloric	hydrochloric
hidyus	hideous
hieght	height
hiepathetical	hypothetical
hier	*higher, hire*
hietus	hiatus
hifinated	hyphenated
higharchy	hierarchy
hijean	hygiene
hijenic	hygienic
himn	*him, hymn*
himoraj	hemorrhage
hindrence	hindrance
hinj	hinge
hiperboly	hyperbole
hipercard	hypercard
hipercritical	*hypercritical*
hiperdermic	hypodermic
hipertenshun	hypertension
hipertext	hypertext
hipie	*hippie, hippy*
hipnosis	hypnosis
hipnotize	hypnotize
hipocrasy	hypocrisy
hipodermic	hypodermic
hipokondria	hypochondria
hipokrit	hypocrite
hipopotamus	hippopotamus
hipothesiss	hypothesis
hipothetical	hypothetical
hippe	*hippie, hippy*
hiprocrit	hypocrite
hirling	hireling

The asterisk (*) next to boldface words flags "misspellings" that are also real words. For words that appear in italics, see Part II, "Sound-Alikes and Confusibles," to confirm your word choice.

WRONG	RIGHT
hiroglyfics	hieroglyphics
histarea	hysteria
histerectomy	hysterectomy
histeria	hysteria
histericks	hysterics
historacal	historical
histreeonics	histrionics
hite	height
hiten	heighten
Hizpanic	Hispanic
hoes*	*hose*
hohm	*home*
hohp	*hoop*
hol	*hole, whole*
holacaust	holocaust
holaday	holiday
holandays	hollandaise
hold*	*holed*
holeness	holiness
holesale	wholesale
holidaies	holidays
holsteen	Holstein
holy*	*holey, wholly*
homaly	*homily*
homanim	homonym
home stretch	homestretch
homiside	homicide
homless	homeless
homly	*homely*
homojeanyus	homogeneous
homojenize	homogenize
homy	*homey*
Honalulu	Honolulu
hoolagan	hooligan

WRONG	RIGHT
hoonta	junta
hopeing	hoping
hor	*hoar, hoer, whore*
horazontally	horizontally
horce	*hoarse, horse*
hord	*hoard, horde, whored*
horderves	hors d'oeuvres
hore	*hoar, hoer, whore*
horrabul	horrible
hors	*hoarse, horse*
hortaculture	horticulture
hos	*hoes, hose*
hospatality	hospitality
hospis	hospice
hospittable	hospitable
hostal	*hostel*
hosury	hosiery
hovle	hovel
hown	*hone*
howrs	*hours, ours*
hox	hoax
hueg	huge
hueman	*human*
humador	humidor
humain	*humane*
humbrage	umbrage
humerous	*humerus, humorous*
hundreth	hundredth
hurdul	hurdle
hurra	hurrah
hutzpa	chutzpah
huzband	husband
hyasinth	hyacinth
hybiscus	hibiscus

WRONG	RIGHT	WRONG	RIGHT
hyde	*hide, hied*	**ignious**	igneous
hydralic	hydraulic	**ignishun**	ignition
hydrostatiks	hydrostatics	**igniteable**	ignitable
hyerglycemia	hypoglycemia	**ignorence**	ignorance
hygene	hygiene	**ignorent**	ignorant
hygenist	hygienist	**igwana**	iguana
Hymlick manuver		**ii**	*aye, eye, I*
	Heimlich maneuver	**ikon**	icon
hypocricy	hypocrisy	**ile**	*aisle, isle*
hypoglisemia	hypoglycemia	**iledgeible**	*illegible*
hypokondria	hypochondria	**ilet**	*eyelet*
hyst	heist	**ilett**	*eyelet, islet*
		ilicit	*elicit, illicit*

I

WRONG	RIGHT	WRONG	RIGHT
		ille	*aisle, isle*
		illegable	*illegible*
		illiterecy	illiteracy
ial	*aisle, isle*	**illojical**	illogical
iatollah	ayatollah	**ilumanate**	illuminate
ich	itch	**ilusion**	*illusion*
icycle	icicle	**ilusive**	*illusive*
idal	*idle, idol, idyll*	**ilustrate**	illustrate
ideeology	*ideology*	**imaculate**	immaculate
ideeya	idea	**imajinary**	imaginary
idel	*ideal, idle, idol, idyll*	**imajination**	imagination
identacal	identical	**imanent**	*eminent, immanent,*
identafy	identify		*imminent*
identifacation	identification	**imatate**	imitate
ideosincracy	idiosyncrasy	**imbacell**	imbecile
idiosy	idiocy	**imbalm**	embalm
idolatrus	idolatrous	**imbalmer**	embalmer
idoll	*idle, idol, idyll*	**imbankment**	embankment
ieland	island	**imbarass**	embarrass
ignaramus	ignoramus	**imbargo**	embargo

The asterisk (*) next to boldface words flags "misspellings" that are also real words. For words that appear in italics, see Part II, "Sound-Alikes and Confusibles," to confirm your word choice.

WRONG	RIGHT
imbark .... embark
imbellish .... embellish
imber .... ember
imbezzle .... embezzle
imbitter .... embitter
imblem .... emblem
imbodied .... embodied
imbolism .... embolism
imboss .... emboss
imbrace .... embrace
imbreo .... embryo
imbroider .... embroider
imbroil .... embroil
imediate ....immediate
imense .... immense
imerge .... *emerge, immerge*
imfasema .... emphysema
imfatic .... emphatic
imformative .... informative
imigrant .... *emigrant*
imigrate .... *emigrate*
iminent .... *eminent, immanent,*
imminent
imissary .... emissary
imitater .... imitator
immagrant .... *immigrant*
immagrate .... *immigrate*
immediatly .... immediately
immpunity .... *impunity*
immunise ....immunize
imobalize .... immobilize
imobile .... immobile
imoral .... *immoral*
imortal .... *immortal*

WRONG	RIGHT
impaneled .... empaneled
impare .... impair
imparshal .... impartial
impasable .... *impassable*
impashence .... impatience
impasible .... *impassible*
impass .... impasse
impatus .... impetus
impecable .... impeccable
impechueus ....impetuous
impedament .... impediment
impeed .... impede
impeereal .... imperial
impekable .... impeccable
impenatrable ....impenetrable
imperitive .... imperative
impertinance ....impertinence
impertinant .... impertinent
impewn .... *impugn*
impewning ....impugning
impewnity ....*impunity*
imphasis .... emphasis
impinj .... impinge
implament .... implement
implausable .... implausible
implisit .... *implicit*
imploshun ....implosion
imploy .... employ
impoodent .... impudent
importence .... importance
imposible .... *impossible*
impossability .... impossibility
imposter .... impostor
impractacable .... *impracticable*

WRONG	RIGHT	WRONG	RIGHT
impraktical	*impractical*	inconveneince	inconvenience
imprizon	imprison	incorajable	incorrigible
imprompto	impromptu	incounter	encounter
improvasation	improvisation	incourage	encourage
improvize	improvise	incouraging	encouraging
improvment	improvement	incredable	*incredible*
impune	*impugn*	incredjulus	*incredulous*
imunity	*immunity*	increemental	incremental
imutable	immutable	increese	increase
in absensha	in absentia	incroach	encroach
in as much as	inasmuch as	incrusted	encrusted
in memoreyam	in memoriam	incumbancy	incumbency
in route	en route	incumber	encumber
inaccessability	inaccessibility	indafatigable	indefatigable
inaccessable	inaccessible	indagent	*indigent*
inact	enact	indanger	endanger
inadaquacy	inadequacy	Indeana	Indiana
inadvertance	inadvertence	indear	endear
inaleinable	inalienable	indeavor	endeavor
inanamate	inanimate	indefensable	indefensible
inaudable	inaudible	indegestible	indigestible
inaugral	inaugural	indejent	*indigent*
incert	insert	indellible	indelible
inchoir	inquire	indemic	*endemic*
incidently	incidentally	indemnafy	*indemnify*
incling	inkling	indemnety	*indemnity*
inclose	enclose	independant	independent
incloshur	enclosure	independense	*independence*
incombustable	incombustible	indepindents	*independents*
incompatable	incompatible	indescreet	*indiscreet, indiscrete*
inconceivible	inconceivable	indestructable	indestructible
incongrous	incongruous	indiet	*indict, indite*
incontestibility	incontestability	indigestable	indigestible

The asterisk (*) next to boldface words flags "misspellings" that are also real words. For words that appear in italics, see Part II, "Sound-Alikes and Confusibles," to confirm your word choice.

WRONG	RIGHT	WRONG	RIGHT
indignat	*indignant*	infered	inferred
indijenus	*indigenous*	inferstracture	infrastructure
indijestion	indigestion	infineer	engineer
indiscreat	*indiscreet, indiscrete*	inflamability	inflammability
indispensible	indispensable	inflamatory	inflammatory
indite*	indict	inflashun	inflation
inditment	indictment	inflewence	influence
indivijul	individual	influenshal	influential
indorse	endorse	infold	enfold
indorsement	endorsement	inforce	enforce
indowment	endowment	infrakshun	*infraction*
indubittable	indubitable	infrekwent	infrequent
induljense	indulgence	ingage	engage
indurable	endurable	ingender	engender
indurance	endurance	ingrane	ingrain or engrain
indure	endure	ingrave	engrave
industreal	industrial	ingrediant	ingredient
inefectual	ineffectual	ingulf	engulf
ineksorable	inexorable	inhance	enhance
inelajable	ineligible	inhearent	inherent
inep	inept	inheritence	inheritance
ineqwality	inequality	inhooman	*inhuman*
ineqwity	*inequity*	inhumain	*inhumane*
inersha	inertia	inigma	enigma
inervate	*enervate*	inipt	*inapt, inept*
ineshal	initial	iniqwity	*iniquity*
inevatable	inevitable	inishal	initial
inevitible	inevitable	inishative	initiative
infachuwait	infatuate	inisheate	initiate
infallability	infallibility	inital	initial
infallable	infallible	initialise	initialize
infantsy	infancy	injeanous	*ingenious*
infattuation	infatuation	injin	engine
infekt	*infect*	injinuity	ingenuity

WRONG	RIGHT	WRONG	RIGHT
injoy	enjoy	**insentives**	incentives
injunkshun	injunction	**inseption**	inception
injuryes	injuries	**insessant**	incessant
ink jet	inkjet	**inshrine**	enshrine
inkalculble	incalculable	**inshur**	*ensure, insure*
inkandesent	incandescent	**insidence**	*incidence*
inkogneto	incognito	**insident**	incident
inkongruous	incongruous	**insidently**	incidentally
inkorporated	incorporated	**insidents**	*incidents*
inkwire	inquire	**insidyous**	*insidious*
inlarge	enlarge	**insiet**	*incite, insight*
inlighten	enlighten	**insign**	ensign
Innernet	Internet	**insigya**	insignia
innervait	*enervate, innervate*	**insipient**	incipient
innitiate	initiate	**insircle**	encircle
innoculate	inoculate	**insirjant**	insurgent
innoculation	inoculation	**insirmountable**	insurmountable
inoble	ennoble	**insision**	incision
inocents	*innocents*	**insisor**	incisor
inocuous	innocuous	**insistance**	insistence
inosence	*innocence*	**insistant**	insistent
inovative	innovative	**insite**	*incite, insight*
inpashent	impatient	**insnare**	ensnare
inpersonate	impersonate	**insolvant**	*insolvent*
inpound	impound	**insommia**	insomnia
inprove	improve	**insoo**	ensue
inrichment	enrichment	**instagate**	instigate
inroll	enroll	**instalation**	installation
insacklopedia	encyclopedia	**instanse**	*instance*
insashable	insatiable	**instantanous**	instantaneous
inscrutible	inscrutable	**instruck**	instruct
insedently	incidentally	**insuffishency**	insufficiency
insendiary	incendiary	**insuffishent**	insufficient

The asterisk (*) next to boldface words flags "misspellings" that are also real words. For words that appear in italics, see Part II, "Sound-Alikes and Confusibles," to confirm your word choice.

WRONG	*RIGHT*	*WRONG*	*RIGHT*
insurection	insurrection	**intolerence**	intolerance
intagral	integral	**intoxacant**	intoxicant
intagrate	integrate	**intrap**	entrap
intamate	intimate	**intreat**	entreat
intanjable	intangible	**intreeg**	intrigue
integraty	integrity	**intrench**	entrench
intelectual	intellectual	**intrest**	interest
intellagence	intelligence	**introdus**	introduce
intellajable	intelligible	**intrust**	entrust
intellechual	intellectual	**intry**	entry
intelligance	intelligence	**intuishun**	intuition
intence	*intense*	**inturn**	intern
Intenshun	intention	**inuendo**	innuendo
interceed	intercede	**invaygal**	inveigle
interfase	interface	**invenshun**	invention
interfeer	interfere	**inveschature**	investiture
intermitent	intermittent	**investagae**	investigate
interogate	interrogate	**inveyed**	*invade, inveighed*
interpert	*interpret*	**inviegle**	inveigle
interprize	enterprise	**invietro**	in vitro
interragate	interrogate	**invilability**	inviolability
interum	interim	**invilable**	inviolable
interupt	*interrupt*	**invinsable**	invincible
interveened	intervened	**invintory**	inventory
intervenous	intravenous	**invironment**	environment
inthrall	*enthrall, in thrall*	**invoise**	invoice
inthralled	enthralled	**invoy**	envoy
inthusiastic	enthusiastic	**inzime**	enzyme
intimadation	intimidation	**ionazation**	ionization
intir	*enter, inter*	**iradescence**	iridescence
intire	entire	**irasable**	*erasable, irascible*
intirety	entirety	**iratability**	irritability
intitle	entitle	**irational**	irrational
intity	entity	**irbane**	*urbane*

WRONG	RIGHT
ireconsilable	irreconcilable
iredeemable	irredeemable
irefutable	irrefutable
iregularity	irregularity
irelevancy	irrelevancy
irelevant	*irrelevant*
irepressable	irrepressible
iresistable	irresistible
iresponsible	irresponsible
iresponsive	irresponsive
ireverent	*irreverent*
irevocable	irrevocable
irgonomics	ergonomics
irigate	irrigate
iritent	irritant
irne	*earn, erne, urn*
ironacally	ironically
irrascible	*irascible*
irrelavant	*irrelevant*
irresistable	irresistible
irritent	irritant
irupt	errupt
iscalayshun	escalation
italisize	italicize
itinarary/itinary	itinerary
iye	*aye, eye, I*

J

WRONG	RIGHT
jagies	jaggies
jamm	*jam, jamb*
janator	janitor

WRONG	RIGHT
janray	genre
jast	*jest*
jaundis	jaundice
javalin	javelin
jeanus	*genus*
jeanyal	genial
jeanyus	*genius*
jelus	*jealous*
jem	gem
jenatals	genitals
jender	gender
jenerally	generally
jeneric	generic
jenerous	generous
jenes	*genes, jeans*
jenocide	genocide
jenteel	genteel
jentile	*gentile*
jentility	gentility
jentle	*gentle*
jenuine	genuine
jeperdy	jeopardy
jepordize	jeopardize
jeraf	giraffe
jerbul	gerbil
jeriatrics	geriatrics
jernal	journal
Jerusalam	Jerusalem
jestation	gestation
jetason	jettison
jewelery	jewelry
jiant	giant
jibberish	gibberish

The asterisk (*) next to boldface words flags "misspellings" that are also real words. For words that appear in italics, see Part II, "Sound-Alikes and Confusibles," to confirm your word choice.

WRONG	RIGHT	WRONG	RIGHT
Jibralta	Gibraltar	juel	jewel
jigalo	gigolo	jueler	jeweler
jigantic	gigantic	juelry	jewelry
jikstapose	juxtapose	juggel	juggle
jimnasium	gymnasium	jugling	juggling
jin	gin	juguler	jugular
jinger	ginger	jujment	judgment
jinjavitis	gingivitis	junkchur	juncture
jinsing	ginseng	junkett	junket
jiroscope	gyroscope	junkshun	junction
jist	*gist*	junyor	junior
jockular	jocular	jurnal	journal
jodpers	jodhpurs	jurney	journey
joging	jogging	justafy	justify
jokeys	jockeys	juvinile	juvenile
jokular	jocular	jyb	*gibe, jibe*
jonkwil	jonquil	jym	gym
joobalant	jubilant		
Joodeism	Judaism		
joojitzu	jujitsu		
jool	jewel		
Joono	Juneau		
Joopater	Jupiter		
joovenile	juvenile		
jossle	jostle		
journnal	journal		
jovyal	jovial		
joyn	join		
joyst	joist		
joyus	joyous		
jubalee	jubilee		
judgement	judgment		
judishall	*judicial*		
judishus	*judicious*		

K

WRONG	RIGHT
kabul	cable
kach	catch
kacki	khaki
kadaver	cadaver
kafateria	cafeteria
kajole	cajole
kalaber	caliber
kalaborator	collaborator
kalaco	calico
Kalafornya	California
kalapers	calipers
kalapse	collapse
kalastomy	colostomy

WRONG	RIGHT	WRONG	RIGHT
kalateral	collateral	kanewing	canoeing
kalender	*calendar, calender*	kannon	*cannon, canon*
kaler	collar	kanope	*canopy*
kaler	color	kanote	connote
kalesterol	cholesterol	kansel	cancel
kalide	collide	kant	*cant, can't*
kalidoscope	kaleidoscope	kantalope	cantaloupe
kalisthenics	callisthenics	Kantuke	Kentucky
kalleeg	colleague	kanvas	*canvas, canvass*
kallvalry	*Calvary, cavalry*	kanyon	canyon
kalm	calm	Kanzes	Kansas
kaloan	cologne	kaos	chaos
kalokweeal	colloquial	kapable	capable
kalonyal	colonial	kapillary	capillary
Kalorado	Colorado	kapital	*capital, capitol*
kalostomy	colostomy	kaptor	captor
kalsium	calcium	karacter	character
kalum	column	karaje	carriage
kamadore	commodore	karanashun	coronation
kamara	camera	karatea	karate
kameo	cameo	karbarator	carburetor
kamiserate	commiserate	kareen	careen
kamodities	commodities	karet	*carat, caret, carrot*
kamoflage	camouflage	karnivorous	carnivorous
kampain	campaign	karode	corrode
kamphor	camphor	karosel	*carousel*
kamune	commune	karoshun	corrosion
kamunicable	communicable	karowse	carouse
kan't	can't	karrot	*carat, caret, carrot*
kanairy	canary	kart blanch	carte blanche
kanapee	*canapé*	karupt	corrupt
kandel	candle	kascade	cascade
Kaneticut	Connecticut	kasem	chasm

The asterisk (*) next to boldface words flags "misspellings" that are also real words. For words that appear in italics, see Part II, "Sound-Alikes and Confusibles," to confirm your word choice.

WRONG	RIGHT	WRONG	RIGHT
kash	cache	kilmat	climate
Kashear	cashier	kilobite	kilobyte
kashoo	cashew	kindergartener	kindergartner
kasm	chasm	kintergarden	kindergarten
kassarole	casserole	Kintucky	Kentucky
kast	*cast*	kirnel	*colonel, kernel*
kastanets	castanets	kiropractor	chiropractor
kastigate	castigate	kitchenet	kitchenette
kasual	*casual*	kizmet	kismet
kataclisum	cataclysm	klack	*clack, claque*
katagorize	categorize	klaranet	clarinet
katapillar	caterpillar	klaws	*Claus, clause, claws*
kataract	cataract	klenz	cleanse
katastrophe	catastrophe	kleracal	clerical
katharsis	catharsis	klik	*click, clique*
katherazation	catheterization	klime	*climb, clime*
katherter	catheter	klimmer	climber
kaushus	cautious	kloke	cloak
kaviar	caviar	kloo	clue
kayotic	chaotic	kloride	chloride
kayson	caisson	klorine	chlorine
ke	*key, quay*	klose	*close, clothes*
kech	ketch	kloths	*cloths*
keemotherapy	chemotherapy	kluts	klutz
keesh	quiche	knicknack	knickknack
kemistry	chemistry	knowledg	knowledge
kemono	kimono	knuckel	knuckle
kepad	keypad	koagulate	coagulate
kerchif	kerchief	koem	comb
kernle	*colonel, kernel*	koema	*coma*
kibits	*kibitz*	koerce	coerce
kiboots	*kibbutz*	koeus	copious
kil	*kill*	kognishun	*cognition*
kilameter	kilometer	koherent	coherent

WRONG	RIGHT	WRONG	RIGHT
koin	*coin, quoin*	konfidante	*confidante*
koinside	coincide	konfident	*confident*
koinsident	coincident	konfigurashun	configuration
koko	cocoa	konfirmation	*confirmation*
kol	*coal, cole, kohl*	konfiscate	confiscate
kolander	*colandar, colander*	konfluence	confluence
kolera	cholera	konformation	*conformation*
kollage	*collage, college*	konglomerate	conglomerate
kolusion	*collusion*	kongregational	congregational
koma	*coma, comma*	konjoin	conjoin
komatose	comatose	konjugate	conjugate
komend	*commend*	konjunktion	conjunction
komical	*comical*	konkomitant	concomitant
komma	*coma, comma*	konkwest	conquest
kompanyon	companion	konosur	connoisseur
kompatable	compatible	konseat	conceit
kompetence	*competence*	konseed	concede
kompetensy	*compentency*	konseeve	conceive
komplaysense	*complacence, complaisance*	konsekwent	consequent
		konsentrate	concentrate
kompliment	*complement, compliment*	konservatory	conservatory
		konshence	*conscience*
komponent	component	konshus	*conscious*
kompozit	composite	konsirvatism	conservatism
komprize	comprise	konsirvatory	conservatory
kompulshun	compulsion	konsistancy	consistency
komputer	computer	konsolashun	consolation
komulsory	compulsory	konsolidashun	consolidation
komunizm	communism	konsonant	consonant
konclushun	conclusion	konsoom	consume
konduit	conduit	konspirator	conspirator
konference	conference	konstellashun	constellation
konfidant	*confidant*		

WRONG	RIGHT
konstitushunality .... constitutionality	
konstraint .... constraint	
konstrucshun .... construction	
konsul ..... *consul, counsel, council*	
konsumable .... consumable	
konsumay .... consommé	
kontajus .... *contagious*	
kontaminating .... contaminating	
kontiguous .... *contiguous*	
kontinjency .... contingency	
kontinual .... *continual*	
kontinuance .... continuance	
kontinues .... *continues*	
kontinuity .... continuity	
kontinuum .... continuum	
kontradict .... contradict	
kontraseptiv .... contraceptive	
kontributory .... contributory	
kontrition .... contrition	
konvayor .... conveyor	
konveenyence .... convenience	
konvenshun .... convention	
konversashun .... conversation	
konvertable .... convertible	
konvicshun .... conviction	
konvivyal .... convivial	
koo .... *coo, coup*	
kooger .... cougar	
kool .... cool	
koop .... *coop, coupe*	
koopon .... coupon	
koordinate .... coordinate	
kor .... *cor, core, corps*	

WRONG	RIGHT
koral .... *choral, corral*	
Koranado .... Coronado	
koranet .... coronet	
kord .... *chord, chored*	
kork .... cork	
kornea .... cornea	
korogate .... corrugate	
koronaries .... coronaries	
koronary .... coronary	
korporal .... *corporal*	
korpse .... *corpse*	
korral .... *choral, corral*	
korrd .... *chord, cord, cored*	
korrespondents ... *correspondents*	
korse .... *coarse, course*	
koshur .... kosher	
kotary .... coterie	
kottage .... cottage	
kounselor ... *councillor, counselor*	
kountenance .... countenance	
koup .... *coo, coup*	
koyn .... *coin, quoin*	
kozmetic .... cosmetic	
kozmic .... cosmic	
kozy .... cosy	
kraft* .... *craft, kraft*	
krall .... crawl	
krane .... crane	
kranyal .... cranial	
krash .... crash	
krate .... crate	
krave .... crave	
kraven .... craven	
krayon .... crayon	

WRONG	RIGHT	WRONG	RIGHT
kraze	craze	kum louday	cum laude
kreak	*creak, creek*	kummerbun	cummerbund
kreashun	creation	kuntree	country
kreate	create	kupon	coupon
kreative	creative	kupul	couple
kredance	credence	kurfew	curfew
kredit	credit	kurser	*curser, cursor*
kreditable	*creditable*	kurtasy	courtesy
kreek	*creak, creek*	kurtyus	courteous
kreem	*cream, crème*	kurvachur	curvature
kreep	creep	kustom	*custom*
kremate	cremate	Kwabec	Quebec
krinj	cringe	kwadrent	quadrant
kript	crypt	kwagmire	quagmire
kriptic	cryptic	kwaifer	quaver
krisalis	chrysalis	kwam	qualm
krisanthanum	chrysanthemum	kwantite	quantity
Krischan	Christian	kwarrel	quarrel
kriteria	criteria	kwarter	quarter
krokadile	crocodile	kwash	quash
kromaic	chromatic	kwayzar	quasar
krome	chrome	kweery	query
kronacle	chronicle	kwell	quell
kronic	chronic	kwench	quench
kronolojacal	chronological	kwery	query
kruel	*crewe, cruel*	kweschun	question
kruks	crux	kweschunair	questionnaire
krusade	crusade	kwest	quest
kruse	*crews, cruise*	kwibble	quibble
kue	*cue, queue*	kwick	quick
kukumber	cucumber	kwiesense	quiescence
kul-de-sac	cul-de-sac	kwiet	quiet
kulpable	culpable	kwip	quip

The asterisk (*) next to boldface words flags "misspellings" that are also real words. For words that appear in italics, see Part II, "Sound-Alikes and Confusibles," to confirm your word choice.

WRONG	RIGHT
kwire	*choir, quire*
kwirk	quirk
kwiter	quitter
kwiver	quiver
kwiz	quiz
kwizzacal	quizzical
kworum	quorum
kwoshent	quotient
kwota	quota
kwotashun	quotation
kwote	quote

L

WRONG	RIGHT
laath	*lath*
labarinth	labyrinth
labelled	labeled
laboror	laborer
labratory	*laboratory*
labul	label
lach	latch
lacker	lacquer
lacksidaisical	lackadaisical
lade*	*laid*
laf	laugh
lafter	laughter
laid*	*lade*
lainth	length
lainthwize	lengthwise
laker	lacquer
lakey	lackey
lakluster	lackluster
laks	*lacks, lax*

WRONG	RIGHT
lam*	*lamb*
lama	llama
lambast	lambaste
lan	*lain, lane*
lanch	launch
langer	languor
langwage	language
langwishing	languishing
lanjeray	lingerie
lankor	languor
lanscape	landscape
lanse	lance
lanturn	lantern
lap top	laptop
laps*	*lapse*
larinjitis	laryngitis
larnix	larynx
larseny	larceny
laserate	lacerate
lasing	lacing
lasirate	lacerate
lasivious	lascivious
latatude	latitude
latint	latent
latis	lattice
latreen	latrine
lattir	*latter*
laurul	laurel
lavendar	lavender
laviathan	leviathan
lavratory	*lavatory*
lawnch	launch
lay*	*lei*
layd	*lade, laid*

WRONG	RIGHT	WRONG	RIGHT
layn	*lain, lane*	**lejer**	ledger
layter	*later*	**lejislashur**	*legislature*
laythe	*lathe*	**lejislates**	legislates
layzay fair	laissez faire	**lejislation**	legislation
laz	*lays, laze*	**lejitamize**	legitimize
lazer	laser	**lejunaire**	legionnaire
leac	*leak, leek*	**leksacon**	lexicon
leanyence	lenience	**lemen**	lemon
leanyent	lenient	**lemited**	limited
leasd	*leased, least*	**lemoseen**	limousine
leasee	lessee	**lene**	*lean, lien*
leason	liaison	**lenth**	length
leasor	lessor	**lenthy**	lengthy
leathal	lethal	**lenz**	*lends, lens*
lecherus	lecherous	**leperd**	leopard
ledgible	*legible*	**lepracy**	leprosy
leding	leading	**lept**	leapt
lee*	*lea*	**lerey**	leery
leeazon	liaison	**lern**	learn
leec	*leak, leek*	**lesee**	lessee
leef	*leaf, lief*	**lesen**	*lessen, lesson*
leeg	league	**lesor**	lessor
leen	*lean, lien*	**lesst**	*lest*
leest	*leased, least*	**lesure**	leisure
lefe	*leaf, lief*	**lethargee**	lethargy
legel	legal	**letharjic**	lethargic
leggasy	legacy	**lether**	leather
legionaire	legionnaire	**levatashun**	levitation
legislater	*legislator, legislature*	**levaty**	levity
legitamate	legitimate	**leve**	*levee, levy*
legoom	legume	**leven**	leaven
leiutenant	lieutenant	**levie**	*levee, levy*
lejable	*legible*	**levrage**	leverage

The asterisk (*) next to boldface words flags "misspellings" that are also real words. For words that appear in italics, see Part II, "Sound-Alikes and Confusibles," to confirm your word choice.

WRONG	RIGHT	WRONG	RIGHT
lew	lieu	linch	lynch
ley	*lay, lei*	lincs	*links, lynx*
leys	*lays, laze*	linedge	*linage, lineage*
lezur	leisure	lingwist	linguist
li	*lie, lye*	lingwistic	linguistic
liabel	*liable*	linial	*lineal*
libary	library	linin	linen
libel*	liable	linnage	*linage, lineage*
libralism	liberalism	linnament	*lineament, liniment*
librarean	librarian	linolyum	linoleum
libul	*libel*	lins	*lens*
licen	*lichen, liken*	linyar	*linear*
licence	license	liquify	liquefy
licer	*licker, liquor*	lire	*liar, lyre*
licorish	licorice	liric	lyric
licure	liqueur	lise	lice
lieable	*liable*	lisense	license
liebel	*libel*	lissen	listen
lieing	lying	litening	*lightening*
lienament	*lineament*	literjy	liturgy
liesure	leisure	litning	*lightning*
lieutenent	lieutenant	litrature	literature
likin	*liken, lichen*	litteral	*literal, littoral*
liklihood	likelihood	liveable	livable
likly	likely	livlihood	livelihood
likor	*licker, liquor*	lo*	*low*
likwid	liquid	lobatomy	lobotomy
likwidity	liquidity	lobbyst	lobbyist
likwify	liquefy	locall	*local, locale*
lim	*limb, limn*	lod	*load, lode, lowed*
limated	limited	lofer	loafer
limazeen	limousine	loger	lodger
limf	lymph	logrithm	logarithm
linament	*lineament, liniment*	lojical	logical

WRONG	RIGHT	WRONG	RIGHT
lojistic	logistic	**loyter**	loiter
lojistical	logistical	**loze**	lose
lokal	*local, locale*	**Luaville**	Louisville
loks	*locks, lox*	**lubracate**	lubricate
lokus	*locus, locust*	**lucchurate**	*luxuriate*
lokwashus	loquacious	**lucjuriant**	*luxuriant*
lon	*loan, lone*	**luckchury**	luxury
lonelyness	loneliness	**luckyer**	luckier
lonjatudinal	longitudinal	**lucurious**	*luxurious*
lonjevaty	longevity	**ludacrus**	ludicrous
lonlyness	loneliness	**Lueseana**	Louisiana
lonne	*loan, lone*	**lugage**	luggage
loobracate	lubricate	**lukemia**	leukemia
lood	lewd	**lukshurence**	luxuriance
lookemia	leukemia	**lumber***	*lumbar*
loominary	luminary	**lunchon**	luncheon
loop*	*loupe*	**lunchonette**	luncheonette
loos	*loose, lose*	**luner**	lunar
loot*	*lute*	**lupe**	*looop, loupe*
lootenant	lieutenant	**lutenant**	lieutenant
loqwicity	loquacity	**luver**	louver
lor	*lore, lower*	**ly**	*lie, lye*
Los Anjelez	Los Angeles	**lyar**	*liar, lyre*
loseing	losing	**lym**	*limb, limn*
loth	*loath*	**lynks**	*links, lynx*
lothe	*loathe*		
lothed	loathed		
lottary	lottery		
loveable	lovable		

M

lovly	lovely	**machurashon**	maturation
lowar	*lore, lower*	**madening**	*maddening*
lowd	*load, lode, lowed*	**maebe**	*maybe*
lowts	louts	**maed**	*made, maid*

The asterisk (*) next to boldface words flags "misspellings" that are also real words. For words that appear in italics, see Part II, "Sound-Alikes and Confusibles," to confirm your word choice.

WRONG	RIGHT
mael	*mail, male*
maen	*main, Maine, mane*
maer	*mare, mayor*
magazene	magazine
magnafacation	magnification
magnafy	magnify
magnamanus	magnanimous
magnatude	magnitude
magnayt	*magnate, magnet*
magnifacent	*magnificent*
magnit	*magnate, magnet*
magot	maggot
mahagony	mahogany
maintnance	maintenance
maise	*maize, maze*
majastrates	magistrates
majic	magic
majishuns	magicians
majoraty	majority
makadamia	macadamia
makarel	mackerel
makaroni	macaroni
Makavelli	Machiavelli
makintosh	*Macintosh, mackintosh, McIntosh*
makro	*macro*
makroscopic	*macroscopic*
maladiction	malediction
malajusted	maladjusted
malarea	malaria
malavolence	malevolence
maleable	malleable
malelovance	malevolence
malfeesence	malfeasance

WRONG	RIGHT
malignent	malignant
maline	malign
malise	malice
malishus	malicious
manacure	manicure
manafest	manifest
manafestatio	manifestation
manafold	manifold
managable	manageable
managment	management
manajerial	managerial
manakin	manikin or mannequin
manar	*manner, manor*
mandrell	*mandrel, mandrill*
manepulation	manipulation
maner	*manner, manor*
manewver	maneuver
manilla	manila
manogamy	monogamy
mans	*man's, manse*
manshun	mansion
mantell	*mantel, mantle*
mantenense	maintenance
manuer	manure
manufacurer	manufacturer
manuver	maneuver
Maraland	Maryland
maranade	marinade
marascino	maraschino
maratal	*marital*
marawana	marijuana
marbul	marble
marderdom	martyrdom
mareeanett	marionette

WRONG	RIGHT
maretal	*marital*
marij	marriage
marjin	margin
markdoun	markdown
markee	marquee
marragable	marriageable
marrage	marriage
marrie	*marry, merry*
marrital	*marital*
marshel/marshil	*marshal, martial*
marshelled	marshaled
marsoopyal	marsupial
martan	*marten, martin*
martanet	martinet
marter	martyr
marvalous	marvelous
Maryetta	Marietta
mas	*mass*
Masachoosets	Massachusetts
masaker	massacre
mase	mace
mased	*massed, mast*
masheen	machine
masheenry	machinery
mashetee	machete
mask*	*masque*
maskarade	masquerade
masoleum	mausoleum
masst	*massed, mast*
mat*	*matte*
mateeriel	*material, materiel*
matenay	matinee

WRONG	RIGHT
maternaty	maternity
mathmatics	mathematics
matradee	maitre d'
matreeark	matriarch
matremony	matrimony
matricks	matrix
mattador	matador
maxamization	maximization
maxamize	maximize
maxmum	maximum
mayd	*made, maid*
mayel	*mail, male*
mayer	*mare, mayor*
mayn	*main, Maine, mane*
mayonaise	mayonnaise
maz	*maize, maze*
meanyal	menial
mechanacal	mechanical
mechinism	mechanism
medatate	meditate
meddel	*medal, meddle*
medea	*media*
medeeate	*mediate*
medel	*medal, meddle*
medeor	meteor
medeum	*medium*
medevil	medieval
mediacrity	mediocrity
medioker	mediocre
medisinal	medicinal
medisine	medicine
medlee	medley
medoe	meadow

The asterisk (*) next to boldface words flags "misspellings" that are also real words. For words that appear in italics, see Part II, "Sound-Alikes and Confusibles," to confirm your word choice.

WRONG	RIGHT	WRONG	RIGHT
medyum	*medium*	meshurable	measurable
meedian	*median*	metamorfasis	metamorphosis
meeger	meager	mete*	*meat, meet*
meen	*mean, mien*	metrapolitan	metropolitan
meet*	*meat, mete*	mettal	*metal, mettle*
meezles	measles	Mexacan	Mexican
megabite	megabyte	mezaneen	mezzanine
megahurts	megahertz	mezmerize	mesmerize
melancoly	melancholy	micraphone	microphone
melenoma	melanoma	micrascope	microscope
meleu	milieu	microprocesser	microprocessor
mellodious	melodious	midle	middle
memmento	memento	miet	*might, mite*
memorble	memorable	migrain	migraine
memry	memory	migreat	migrate
memwars	memoirs	mij	midge
menas	menace	mijet	midget
menashuree	menagerie	Mikalanjeo	Michelangelo
meninjitis	meningitis	mikro	*micro*
menstral	menstrual	mikroscopic	*microscopic*
ment	meant	milage	mileage
ments	*mince, mints*	milaner	milliner
menx	*minks, minx*	milatate	militate
merang	meringue	milenium	millennium
meratorious	*meritorious*	milinery	*millenary, millinery*
Mercaree	Mercury	milisha	militia
merchandize	merchandise	militent	militant
meread	myriad	millenneum	millennium
merj	merge	millionair	millionaire
mersaful	merciful	milyew	milieu
mersinary	mercenary	milyon	million
mertrishus	*meretricious*	mimacree	mimicry
mery	*marry, merry*	minachure	miniature
mes	*mess*	minamize	minimize

WRONG	RIGHT	WRONG	RIGHT
minar	*miner, minor*	mitagation	mitigation
Minasota	Minnesota	mizer	miser
mincks	*minks, minx*	mizerable	miserable
mineralojical	mineralogical	Mizuree	Missouri
miniscule	minuscule	moad	*mode, mowed*
minmum	minimum	mocasin	moccasin
minned	*mind, mined*	mockary	mockery
minnuet	minuet	modafy	modify
minoraty	minority	modalaty	modality
minse	*mince, mints*	moddal	*modal, model*
minster	minister	modefacation	modification
minstrul	minstrel	modil	*modal, model*
minusha	minutia	modjular	modular
miraj	mirage	modo	motto
misal	*missal, missle*	modulater	modulator
misalinement	misalignment	moduler	modular
Misasipee	Mississippi	modum	modem
mischevious	mischievous	moed	*mode, mowed*
misconsepshun	misconception	moetif	*motif*
mise	mice	moetiv	*motive*
mised	*missed, mist*	Mohamed	Mohammed
misetro	maestro	moischur	moisture
Mishagan	Michigan	molases	molasses
mishunary	missionary	molekular	molecular
misjuge	misjudge	moler	molar
misle	*missal, missle*	mollafy	mollify
misletoe	mistletoe	moltin	molten
mispell	misspell	mon	*moan, mown*
missellaneous	miscellaneous	monacrome	monochrome
missia	messiah	monagraph	monograph
missnomer	misnomer	monaker	*moniker*
misteryus	mysterious	monarcee	monarchy
mitagate	mitigate	monark	monarch

The asterisk (*) next to boldface words flags "misspellings" that are also real words. For words that appear in italics, see Part II, "Sound-Alikes and Confusibles," to confirm your word choice.

WRONG	RIGHT	WRONG	RIGHT
monastasizm	monasticism	mortafication	mortification
monatary	*monetary*	mortishen	mortician
monator	*monitor*	Moscovite	Muscovite
monatory	*monitory*	moshun	motion
mone	*moan, mown*	moskeetoes	mosquitoes
monemaking	moneymaking	mot	*moat, mote*
monetor	*monitor*	motavate	motivate
mongrul	mongrel	moteef	*motif*
monkeies	monkeys	moter	motor
monnorail	monorail	motlee	motley
monnotnous	monotonous	motoes	mottoes
monocrome	monochrome	motzarella	mozzarella
monokal	monocle	mountin	mountain
monotnous	monotonous	movable	moveable
monseenyer	monsignor	mowse	mouse
Montanna	Montana	mowt	*moat, mote*
Montasori	Montessori	mozaic	mosaic
moocus	*mucous, mucus*	Mozez	Moses
mood*	*mooed*	Mozlem	Moslem
moos	*moose, mousse*	mrtle	myrtle
moot*	*mute*	muchual	*mutual, mutuel*
moov	move	mukus	*mucous, mucus*
moows	*mews, muse*	multipel	multiple
morealaty	*morality*	multymedea	multimedia
morening	*morning, mourning*	multytasking	multitasking
moretality	*mortality*	munifacent	*munificent*
morfeen	morphine	munisapal	municipal
morfing	morphing	munishun	munition
morg	morgue	mur	myrrh
morgage	mortgage	murmer	murmur
morral	*moral*	murning	*morning, mourning*
morrale	*morale*	mus	*mews, muse*
morrs	*moors, Moors, mores*	muscet	*muscat, musket*
morsle	morsel	musel	*muscle, mussel*

WRONG	RIGHT	WRONG	RIGHT
musicle	musical	**nachure**	nature
musketo	mosquito	**nack**	knack
musle	*muscle, mussel*	**nackwurst**	knackwurst
musn't	mustn't	**naeve**	*knave, nave*
musse	*moose, mousse*	**nap***	*knap*
mussle	*muscle, mussel*	**napken**	napkin
must*	*mussed*	**Napolyon**	Napoleon
mustash	mustache	**narative**	narrative
musterd	*mustard, mustered*	**narkotic**	narcotic
mut	*moot, mute*	**narl**	gnarl
mutalate	mutilate	**Narobee**	Nairobi
mutul	*mutual, mutuel*	**narsasism**	narcissism
muzacal	musical	**nash**	gnash
muzic	music	**nashun**	nation
muzical	musical	**nat**	gnat
muzishan	musician	**naturaly**	naturally
muzle	*muzzle*	**nausha**	nausea
Muzlim	Muslim	**naut**	*knot, naught, not*
mynd	*mind, mined*	**nautacal**	nautical
mynor	*miner, minor*	**nauty**	*knotty, naughty*
myst	*missed, mist*	**Navada**	Nevada
mystefy	mystify	**navagate**	navigate
mysteryous	mysterious	**Navaho**	Navajo
myte	*might, mite*	**nave***	*knave*
mythalogical	mythological	**navil**	*naval, navel*
		naw	gnaw

N

WRONG	RIGHT	WRONG	RIGHT
		nawt	*knot, naught*
		naybor	neighbor
		nazal	nasal
na	*nay, neigh*	**nead**	knead
Nabraska	Nebraska	**necesarily**	necessarily
Naches	Natchez	**necesary**	necessary
nachural	natural	**necesity**	necessity

The asterisk (*) next to boldface words flags "misspellings" that are also real words. For words that appear in italics, see Part II, "Sound-Alikes and Confusibles," to confirm your word choice.

WRONG	RIGHT
neckter	nectar
neecap	kneecap
Neechee	Nietzsche
need*	*knead, kneed*
neel	kneel
neerby	nearby
neese	niece
neether	*neither*
nefew	nephew
neglajable	negligible
negoshiat	negotiate
negoshible	negotiable
neice	niece
neid	*knead, kneed, need*
neih	*nay, neigh*
nell	knell
nelt	knelt
nemasis	nemesis
nemonick	mnemonic
neofite	neophyte
nervus	nervous
nesessary	necessary
nesessity	necessity
nether*	neither
New Hampshur	New Hampshire
New Jerzey	New Jersey
New Meksaco	New Mexico
New Yourk	New York
new*	*knew*
newclear	nuclear
newmatic	pneumatic
newmonia	pneumonia
newrotic	neurotic
newtral	neutral

WRONG	RIGHT
newz	news
ney	*née*
neyther	*neither, nether*
neyv	*knave, nave*
ni	nigh
niasin	niacin
Nicaragwa	Nicaragua
nich	niche
nickle	nickel
nicknack	knickknack
nieghbor	neighbor
niet	*knight, night*
niether	*neither*
nieve	naive
nife	knife
nimbul	nimble
nimf	nymph
nineth	ninth
ninetyth	ninetieth
ninteen	nineteen
ninty	ninety
nisateas	niceties
nise	nice
nit*	*knit*
nite	*knight, night*
nitrajin	nitrogen
nitrogliserin	nitroglycerin
no*	*know*
noad	node
nob*	*knob*
nobby	knobby
noch	notch
nock	knock
noes*	*knows, nose*

WRONG	RIGHT	WRONG	RIGHT
nokshus	noxious	**nown**	known
nokturnal	nocturnal	**noxyus**	noxious
noledge	knowledge	**noyseless**	noiseless
noll	knoll	**ntreent**	nutrient
nomanal	nominal	**nuckle**	knuckle
nomanate	nominate	**nudaty**	nudity
nome	gnome	**nuer**	neuter
nomenklachur	nomenclature	**nuj**	nudge
nomine	nominee	**numaric**	numeric
non sekwetur	non sequitur	**nummerable**	numerable
nonpartasan	nonpartisan	**numness**	numbness
nonrefundible	nonrefundable	**numonia**	pneumonia
nonshalant	nonchalant	**nun***	*none*
noo	*knew, new*	**nupial**	nuptial
nooron	neuron	**nurchur**	nurture
noos	news	**nurological**	neurological
noovo rich	nouveau riche	**nuron**	neuron
normalazation	normalization	**nurosis**	neurosis
North Dacota	North Dakota	**nurotic**	neurotic
North Karalina	North Carolina	**nursree**	nursery
nos	*knows, noes, nose*	**nusance**	nuisance
noshun	notion	**nutrality**	neutrality
nostalja	nostalgia	**nutron**	neutron
not*	*knot*		
notafying	notifying		
notarise	notarize		
notess	notice		
notiry	notary	**o**	*oh, owe*
notisable	noticeable	**Oaklahoma**	Oklahoma
notoreus	notorious	**oar***	*ore*
notority	notoriety	**obedeent**	obedient
notoryus	notorious	**obees**	obese
notty	*knotty, naughty*	**obichuary**	obituary

O

The asterisk (*) next to boldface words flags "misspellings" that are also real words. For words that appear in italics, see Part II, "Sound-Alikes and Confusibles," to confirm your word choice.

WRONG	RIGHT	WRONG	RIGHT
objektives	objectives	ofense	offense
oblagations	obligations	ofer	offer
obleek	oblique	offence	offense
oblij	oblige	offishal	official
oblitarate	obliterate	offishate	officiate
obliveon	oblivion	offline	off-line
obnokshus	obnoxious	ofice	office
obsalesence	obsolescence	oficer	officer
obsalesent	obsolescent	ofishal	official
obsalete	obsolete	ofishus	officious
obscoor	obscure	ofthalmoscope	ophthalmoscope
obseen	obscene	oh*	*owe*
observent	observant	Ohyo	Ohio
obstacal	obstacle	OK*	okay
obstatrishan	obstetrician	oke	oak
ocasion	occasion	okey	okay
ocasional	occasional	oktane	octane
ocationally	occasionally	oktapus	octopus
occation	occasion	okupie	occupy
occationally	occasionally	olagarkey	oligarchy
occupent	occupant	oleeo	*oleo, olio*
occured	occurred	om	ohm
occurence	occurrence	omelet	omelet
ocult	occult	ominus	ominous
ocupant	occupant	omision	*omission*
ocupy	occupy	omited	omitted
ocur	occur	omiting	omitting
ocurred	occurred	omitt	omit
ocurrence	occurrence	ommission	*omission*
ocurring	occurring	omnabus	omnibus
od	*ode, owed*	omnipotance	omnipotence
odderiferus	odoriferous	onararium	honorarium
oder	odor	onarary	honorary
ofend	offend	onerable	honorable

WRONG	RIGHT	WRONG	RIGHT
onerus	onerous	orcestrate	orchestrate
onery	ornery	orcherd	orchard
onesself	oneself	ordar	*order, ordure*
online	on-line	ordenarily	ordinarily
onse	*once*	ordenary	ordinary
Ontareo	Ontario	orderleness	orderliness
onyon	onion	orderves	hors d'oeuvres
opayk	opaque	ordinence	*ordinance*
openion	opinion	ordinnal	ordinal
operater	operator	ordnence	*ordnance*
opinyon	opinion	oreent	orient
oportunity	opportunity	oreentate	orientate
oposite	*opposite*	orental	oriental
opreble	operable	oreole	oriole
opreshun	oppression	orfan	orphan
optacul	optical	orfanaj	orphanage
optamism	optimism	organazation	organization
optamist	optimist	originel	original
optamum	optimum	orijin	origin
opthamology	ophthalmology	orijinal	original
opthamolagist	ophtalmologist	orjee	orgy
optimise	optimize	orkestra	orchestra
opulance	opulence	ornamint	ornament
opulant	opulent	ornathology	ornithology
or*	*oar*	orotory	oratory
oracel	*oracle*	Orregon	Oregon
oraculer	oracular	orthadonics	orthodontics
orafis	orifice	orthadox	orthodox
oragin	origin	orthapedic	orthopedic
orall	*aural, oral*	osillate	*oscillate*
orangatang	orangutan	osillation	oscillation
oratoracal	oratorical	oskulate	*osculate*
orbatal	orbital	ossafi	ossify

The asterisk (*) next to boldface words flags "misspellings" that are also real words. For words that appear in italics, see Part II, "Sound-Alikes and Confusibles," to confirm your word choice.

WRONG	RIGHT	WRONG	RIGHT
osteej	ostrich	pael	*pail, pale*
ostensable	ostensible	pagent	pageant
ostintashun	ostentation	painsteaking	painstaking
ostrasize	ostracize	pait	pate
ostrasizm	ostracism	pajent	pageant
ouht	*aught, ought*	pajination	pagination
outmanuver	outmaneuver	pak	pack
outrageus	outrageous	Pakastan	Pakistan
outway	outweigh	paked	*packed, pact*
overceas	*overseas, oversees*	paladium	palladium
overdo*	*overdue*	palashal	palatial
overite	overwrite	palet	*palate, palette, pallet*
overlaping	overlapping	paliss	palace
oversees*	*overseas*	paller	pallor
overwelmed	overwhelmed	pallushun	pollution
ovreseas	*overseas*	palpait	*palpate*
owd	*ode, owed*	palpatate	*palpitate*
owenership	ownership	palse	*pause, paws*
owrs	*hours, ours*	palute	pollute
oxadashun	oxidation	palzy	palsy
oxajen	oxygen	pamento	pimento
ozmosis	osmosis	pamflet	pamphlet
		panaling	paneling
		panalist	panelist

P

WRONG	RIGHT	WRONG	RIGHT
		panarama	panorama
		panash	panache
		pandamonium	pandemonium
pac	*pack, pact*	panik	panic
pacafy	pacify	paniky	panicky
pach	patch	paparus	papyrus
pacifie	pacify	paper mashay	papier-mâché
packaderm	pachyderm	paperwate	paperweight
pade	paid	par excelanz	par excellence
padek	paddock	parabul	parable
padestrian	pedestrian		

WRONG	RIGHT	WRONG	RIGHT
paradee	parody	**parrallel**	parallel
paradice	paradise	**parrish**	*parish, perish*
paradime	paradigm	**parrity**	parity
parafenalia	paraphernalia	**parsamonious**	parsimonious
paralasis	paralysis	**parsel**	*parcel*
paralegle	paralegal	**parshal**	*partial*
paralell	parallel	**parsly**	parsley
paralisis	paralysis	**partacle**	particle
paralyse	paralyze	**partasan**	partisan
paramont	paramount	**partasipul**	participle
paramutual	parimutuel	**Parthanon**	Parthenon
parapatetic	peripatetic	**particapate**	participate
paraphenalia	paraphernalia	**participent**	participant
parapleejic	paraplegic	**particuler**	particular
parashoot	parachute	**particulerly**	particularly
parden	pardon	**partime**	part-time
pardise	paradise	**partisapate**	participate
pare*	*pear*	**partisapated**	participated
pareable	parable	**partisapation**	participation
parearch	patriarch	**partishun**	*partition*
pareil	peril	**partisipant**	participant
parfay	parfait	**partisiple**	participle
paria	pariah	**partizan**	partisan
parikeet	parakeet	**partrige**	partridge
parkay	parquet	**pasay**	passé
parla	*parlay*	**paschur**	pasture
parlament	parliament	**paschurize**	pasteurize
parlee	*parley*	**pased**	*passed, past*
parler	parlor	**paser**	pacer
parliment	parliament	**pashense**	*patience, patients*
parly	*parley*	**pashun**	passion
parokeal	parochial	**Pasific**	Pacific
paroll	*parol, parole*	**passinger**	passenger

The asterisk (*) next to boldface words flags "misspellings" that are also real words. For words that appear in italics, see Part II, "Sound-Alikes and Confusibles," to confirm your word choice.

WRONG	RIGHT
passtime	pastime
past*	*passed*
pastle	pastel
pastorle	pastoral
pasttime	pastime
pasturize	pasteurize
pasword	password
patant	patent
patay	paté
pateet	*petite*
paternaty	paternity
pathalogy	pathology
pathatic	pathetic
pathelojacal	pathological
patint	patent
patrishen	patrician
patroling	patrolling
paty	patty
paus	*pause, paws*
pavillion	pavilion
pawsity	paucity
payj	page
payl	*pail, pale*
payn	*pain, pane*
payr	*pair, pare*
paysed	*paced, paste*
payshents	*patience, patients*
paytrons	patrons
pazley	paisley
peacable	peaceable
peano	piano
pearish	*parish, perish*
peasent	peasant
peculyar	peculiar

WRONG	RIGHT
pedagojacal	pedagogical
pedagree	pedigree
pedastul	pedestal
peddal	*pedal, peddle, petal*
pedeatric	pediatric
pedeatrishan	pediatrician
pedle	*pedal. peddle, petal*
peece	*peace, piece*
peek*	*peak, pique*
peekoe	pekoe
peel*	*peal*
peenuckle	pinochle
peeon	*paean, peon*
peepul	people
peer*	*pier*
peeramid	pyramid
peese	*peace, piece*
peetishun	*petition*
pekooyar	peculiar
pelacan	pelican
penanse	penance
penant	pennant
penasillan	penicillin
penatense	penitence
penatenshearies	penitentiaries
penatenshery	penitentiary
penatent	penitent
penatrate	penetrate
penatration	penetration
pencil*	*pensile*
pendalum	pendulum
pendent*	*pendant*
penelty	penalty
penence	penance

WRONG	RIGHT
penicilin	penicillin
pennaless	penniless
penndent	*pendant, pendent*
pennent	pennant
pennywait	pennyweight
penshun	pension
pensill	*pencil, pensile*
Pensilvania	Pennsylvania
Penteum	Pentium
penuckle	pinochle
per anum	per annum
per deeum	per diem
per say	per se
per*	*purr*
peral	peril
perameter	*parameter, perimeter*
percalator	percolator
perceptable	perceptible
percieve	perceive
perclude	preclude
percushun	percussion
perdict	predict
perdishun	perdition
pereferal	peripheral
peremtory	*peremptory*
pereneyal	perennial
pereodical	periodical
perepheral	peripheral
perfec	*perfect*
perferable	preferable
performence	performance
periferal	peripheral
perifery	periphery

WRONG	RIGHT
perimater	*parameter, perimeter*
perishible	perishable
perkolate	percolate
perl	*pearl, purl*
permanance	permanence
permanant	permanent
permisible	permissible
pernishus	pernicious
pernounce	pronounce
pernunciation	pronunciation
perogative	prerogative
perpare	prepare
perparedness	preparedness
perpatrate	*perpetrate*
perpatuity	perpetuity
perpechuate	*perpetuate*
perpechuly	perpetually
perpendiculer	perpendicular
perponderanc	preponderance
perport	purport
perpose	*purpose*
perposterus	preposterous
perril	peril
perscription	prescription
perseecute	*persecute*
persenal	*personal*
persenality	*personality*
personnel	*personnel*
persent	percent
perseptable	perceptible
perseption	perception
perseptive	*perceptive*
perseptual	perceptual

The asterisk (*) next to boldface words flags "misspellings" that are also real words. For words that appear in italics, see Part II, "Sound-Alikes and Confusibles," to confirm your word choice.

WRONG	RIGHT
perservative	preservative
perserve	preserve
perseverense	perseverance
Pershan	Persian
persipitation	precipitation
persise	precise
persistant	persistent
persnalty	*personalty*
persnickaty	persnickety
persoena non grata	persona non grata
personafy	personify
personalaty	*personality*
personel	*personal, personnel*
persuaid	persuade
persuance	pursuance
persuant	pursuant
persuation	persuasion
persue	*peruse, pursue*
persuent	persuant
persuit	pursuit
persumchus	presumptuous
persume	presume
perswade	persuade
perswasion	persuasion
perswasive	persuasive
pertinance	pertinence
perus	*peruse*
pervaricate	prevaricate
perview	purview
peschalence	pestilence
pesentry	peasantry
pestaside	pesticide
pestilance	pestilence

WRONG	RIGHT
petagog	pedagogue
petefor	petit four
petision	*petition*
petrafy	petrify
petrolleum	petroleum
pettal	*pedal, peddle, petal*
petulence	petulance
petulent	petulant
pety	*petty*
pewny	puny
pewtrify	putrefy
peyon	*paean, peon*
peyst	*paced, paste*
phaze	*faze, phase*
Pheenix	Phoenix
phillter	*filter, philter*
philosphy	philosophy
phisician	physician
phizz	*fizz, phiz*
phlocks	*flocks, phlox*
physisian	physician
pi*	*pie*
picalo	piccolo
pich	pitch
pichur	*pitcher*
pickchuress	*picturesque*
picknicking	picnicking
picksel	pixel
pidjin	*pidgin, pigeon*
pieity	piety
pier*	*peer*
pijon	*pidgin, pigeon*
pikaresk	*picaresque*
Pikaso	Picasso

WRONG	RIGHT	WRONG	RIGHT
pikchur	*picture*	**pisstol**	*pistil, pistol*
pikchuresk	*picturesque*	**pistasheo**	pistachio
pikel	pickle	**pistel**	*pistil, pistol*
piket	picket	**pitable**	*pitiable*
piknik	picnic	**pitaful**	*pitiful*
piksy	*pixie, pyxie*	**pitaless**	pitiless
piktoral	pictorial	**pitance**	pittance
pillaj	pillage	**Pitsburg**	Pittsburgh
pillary	pillory	**pittence**	pittance
piller	pillar	**pitty**	pity
pillfer	pilfer	**pituatary**	pituitary
pillgrim	pilgrim	**pityful**	*pitiful*
pillo	pillow	**pityous**	piteous
pindant	*pendant, pendent*	**pivatal**	pivotal
pinnacal	pinnacle	**pivet**	pivot
pinsers	pincers	**piza**	*piazza, pizza*
pinyata	piñata	**plaat**	*plait, plat, plate*
pinyo	pinion	**plag**	plague
pipet	*pipette*	**plagarism**	plagiarism
pirasy	piracy	**plajarise**	plagiarize
pirchase	purchase	**plajarism**	plagiarism
pirite	pyrite	**plak**	plaque
pirl	*pearl, purl*	**planatarium**	planetarium
pirloin	*purloin*	**plane***	*plain, plane*
piroteknik	pyrotechnic	**planetif**	*plaintiff*
pirport	purport	**planetive**	*plaintive*
pirpose	*purpose*	**planit**	planet
pirsuance	pursuance	**planshet**	planchette
pirsuant	pursuant	**plantashun**	plantation
pirsue	pursue	**plantir**	*plantar, planter*
pirsuit	pursuit	**plase**	*place, plaice, plays*
piruzal	perusal	**plasebo**	placebo
pirview	purview	**plasenta**	placenta

The asterisk (*) next to boldface words flags "misspellings" that are also real words. For words that appear in italics, see Part II, "Sound-Alikes and Confusibles," to confirm your word choice.

WRONG	RIGHT	WRONG	RIGHT
plastor	plaster	polatishan	politician
plat*	*plait, plat, plate*	pole*	*Pole, poll*
platapus	platypus	poleese	police
platatude	platitude	poler	polar
platau	plateau	poletry	*poultry*
plated*	*plaited, platted*	poligamy	polygamy
platin	platen	polisee	policy
plato	plateau	politacal	political
plausability	plausibility	politishan	politician
plausable	plausible	pollin	pollen
Playtoe	Plato	pollytheism	polytheism
playwrite	playwright	poltise	poultice
plazma	plasma	poltree	*paltry*
pleaz	*pleas, please*	poltry	*poultry*
plebean	plebeian	pomegranite	pomegranate
pleese	*pleas, please*	pompadoor	pompadour
plej	pledge	pomposaty	pomposity
plerral	*pleural, plural*	pompus	pompous
plesant	pleasant	ponderus	ponderous
pleshur	pleasure	pontifacate	pontificate
plesure	pleasure	popler	*poplar*
plient	pliant	populase	*populace*
plublickly	publicly	populer	*popular*
plum*	*plumb*	populus	*populous*
plurasy	pleurisy	por	*poor, pore, pour*
plurral	*pleural, plural*	Porchugal	Portugal
podeum	podium	poretent	*portent*
poetent	*potent*	porshun	*portion*
pognant	poignant	portfoleo	portfolio
poingnant	poignant	Porto Rico	Puerto Rico
poinsetta	poinsettia	portrayle	portrayal
poizoning	poisoning	portret	portrait
poket	pocket	porus	porous
polacies	policies	poschur	posture

WRONG	RIGHT	WRONG	RIGHT
poscrip	postscript	pranse	prance
posess	possess	praposition	proposition
posession	possession	prarie	prairie
posessive	possessive	prayse	*praise, prays, preys*
posessor	possessor	pre-school	preschool
poshun	*potion*	prearange	prearrange
posibility	possibility	preceed	*precede*
posible	possible	precense	*presence,*
posision	position		*presents*
possability	possibility	precentment	*presentment*
possable	possible	precosity	precocity
possesser	possessor	predesessor	predecessor
possum	opossum	predictible	predictable
postponment	postponement	predjudice	prejudice
potaseum	potassium	preech	preach
potatos	potatoes	preemptorily	peremptorily
potenshal	potential	preemptory*	*peremptory*
potensheality	potentiality	preetest	*pretest*
potery	pottery	preetext	*pretext*
pouerful	powerful	preevent	prevent
powch	pouch	preferance	preference
poyzon	poison	prefered	preferred
pozative	positive	preferenshal	preferential
practicly	practically	preferible	preferable
practise	practice	prefess	preface
pragress	progress	preforate	perforate
praire	prairie	preforation	perforation
prais	*praise, prays, preys*	preform*	*perform*
praject	project	preformance	performance
prakticable	*practicable*	prefrence	preference
praktical	*practical*	prefunctory	perfunctory
praktishuner	practitioner	pregnensy	pregnancy
pramulgate	promulgate	prehaps	perhaps

WRONG	RIGHT
prejudise	prejudice
prekarious	precarious
prekoshus	precocious
prekosity	precocity
premedtate	premeditate
premeer	premier
premeyum	premium
preminent	preeminent
premiss	*premise*
premit	permit
premptory	*peremptory, preemptory*
preparetory	preparatory
prepasition	*preposition, proposition*
preplex	perplex
preponderence	preponderance
presadential	presidential
presadents	*precendence, precedents*
prescripsion	prescription
preseding	*preceding*
preseed	*precede*
presentament	*presentiment*
preshure	pressure
presidence	*precedence, precedents*
presink	precinct
presipatate	precipitate
presipice	precipice
presis	*precis*
presise	*precise*
presisely	precisely
presision	precision

WRONG	RIGHT
preskribe	*prescribe*
prespective	*perspective*
prespiration	perspiration
prestijus	prestigious
presuade	persuade
presuasion	persuasion
presumebly	presumably
presumtion	presumption
pretain	pertain
pretence	pretense
pretenshus	pretentious
preturb	perturb
preturbable	perturbable
pretzle	pretzel
prevade	pervade
prevalant	prevalent
prevasive	pervasive
prexistent	preexistent
prezents	*presence, presents*
prezervasun	preservation
prezerve	preserve
prezide	preside
prezident	president
prezoom	presume
prezumpshun	presumption
primaraly	primarily
primative	primitive
primevil	primeval
primordeal	primordial
prinsapality	principality
prinse	*prince, prints*
prinsess	*princes, princess*
prinsipal	*principal, principle*
printz	*prince, prints*

WRONG	RIGHT	WRONG	RIGHT
privasee	privacy	**projekshun**	projection
privleje	privilege	**projektile**	projectile
priz	*pries, prize*	**proklivity**	proclivity
prizm	prism	**proletarieat**	proletariat
prizon	prison	**prolifick**	prolific
prizoner	prisoner	**prolog**	prologue
probablity	probability	**promanent**	prominent
probablly	probably	**promasory**	promissory
probashun	probation	**promiss**	*promise*
probishun	prohibition	**promt**	prompt
problamatical	problematical	**promtly**	promptly
problim	problem	**pronounse**	pronounce
procede	*proceed*	**pronunsiashun**	pronunciation
procedur	procedure	**prood**	prude
prodagal	prodigal	**proon**	prune
prodeuc	produce	**propasishun**	*preposition,*
prodijus	prodigious		*proposition*
prodoose	produce	**propensaty**	propensity
producable	producible	**prophecyes**	prophecies
profalactic	prophylactic	**propicheate**	propitiate
profer	proffer	**propishus**	propitious
profeshun	profession	**propogate**	propagate
profesi	*prophesy*	**proponant**	proponent
professer	professor	**proporshunal**	proportional
profesy	*prophecy*	**propozal**	proposal
profet	*profit, prophet*	**propoze**	*propose*
proff	proof	**propriatary**	proprietary
proffit	*profit, prophet*	**propriator**	proprietor
profishency	proficiency	**propriaty**	propriety
profushun	profusion	**pros***	*prose*
programed	programmed	**prosedure**	procedure
programing	programming	**proseecute**	*prosecute*
prohabishun	prohibition	**proseed**	*proceed*

The asterisk (*) next to boldface words flags "misspellings" that are also real words. For words that appear in italics, see Part II, "Sound-Alikes and Confusibles," to confirm your word choice.

WRONG	RIGHT	WRONG	RIGHT
proseeding	*proceeding*	pupul	pupil
proseedural	procedural	pur	*per, purr*
prosess	process	purafacation	purification
prosesser	processor	purafied	purified
proskribe	*prescribe, proscribe*	purafy	purify
proslatize	proselytize	puratan	Puritan
prospektive	*prospective*	puraty	purity
prostait	*prostate*	purefication	purification
prostrait	*prostrate*	purj	purge
protacal	protocol	purmeable	permeable
protajay	protégé	purposs	*purpose*
protecshun	protection	purpul	purple
proteen	*protean, protein*	pursuence	pursuance
protestent	Protestant	pursuent	pursuant
protuberence	protuberance	pus*	*puss*
proverhyal	proverbial	putrafakashun	putrefaction
provinshal	provincial	py	*pi, pie*
provishun	provision		
proxamal	proximal		
prudant	prudent		
pruv	prove		
pryde	*pride, pried*		
pryor	prior		
pryse	*pries, prize*		
psichiatry	psychiatry		
psycology	psychology		
publick	public		
publickly	publicly		
pugnashus	pugnacious		
pulverise	pulverize		
punative	punitive		
punjencie	pungency		
punjent	pungent		
punkchul	punctual		

WRONG	RIGHT
quadralateral	quadrilateral
quadraplex	quadruplex
quadraseps	quadriceps
quadrent	quadrant
quadrooped	quadruped
quadruplacate	quadruplicate
quanity	quantity
quarantee	guarantee
quarel	quarrel
que	*cue, queue*
queeried	queried
queery	query
querk	quirk

WRONG	RIGHT
queschun	question
questionarie	questionnaire
quilt	*gilt, guilt*
quinse	quince
quintesenshal	quintessential
quinttillion	quintillion
quintupplet	quintuplet
quited	quitted
quiter	*quitor, quitter*
quizacal	quizzical
quizing	quizzing
quoshent	quotient
quotashun	quotation
qwaf	quaff
qwail	quail
qwalatative	*qualitative*
qwalify	*qualify*
qwantafie	*quantify*
qwantatative	*quantitative*
qwaranteen	quarantine
qwarter	quarter
qwarts	*quarts, quartz*
qwayzar	quasar
qwiet	*quiet*
qwior	*choir, quire*
qwit	*quit*
qwite	*quite*
qwote	quote
qwoting	quoting

R

WRONG	RIGHT
rabit	*rabbet, rabbit*
rack*	*wrack*
racket*	*racquet*
racoon	raccoon
radacal	*radical, radicle*
raddish	*reddish, radish*
rade	*raid, rayed*
radeo	radio
radeus	radius
radiater	radiator
radient	radiant
radyus	radius
raez	*raise, raze*
raign	*rain, reign, rein*
raindeer	reindeer
rainj	range
raion	rayon
raith	*wraith, wrath*
raize	*raise, raze*
raizer	*raiser, razor*
rak	*rack, wrack*
raket	*racket, racquet*
rale*	*rail*
Ralee	Raleigh
ramafacation	ramification
rambul	ramble
rambunkshus	rambunctious
ramshakel	ramshackle
rancer	*rancor, ranker*
randayvu	rendezvous

The asterisk (*) next to boldface words flags "misspellings" that are also real words. For words that appear in italics, see Part II, "Sound-Alikes and Confusibles," to confirm your word choice.

WRONG	RIGHT	WRONG	RIGHT
randomise	randomize	**rayz**	*raise, rays, raze*
rangler	wrangler	**razberry**	raspberry
rankor	*rancor, ranker*	**razer**	*raiser, razor*
rankul	rankle	**reajust**	readjust
ransid	rancid	**reak**	*reek, wreak*
ransum	ransom	**realaty**	*reality, realty*
rap*	*wrap*	**realazashun**	realization
rapchur	rapture	**realety**	*reality, realty*
rapd	*rapped, rapt, wrapped*	**realter**	realtor
rapore	rapport	**rearvew**	rearview
rappt	*rapped, rapt, wrapped*	**rebell**	rebel
rapsody	rhapsody	**rebownd**	*rebound*
rapyer	rapier	**rebutle**	rebuttal
raraty	rarity	**recalsatrant**	recalcitrant
rarbit	*rarebit*	**recalsitrate**	recalcitrate
rarify	rarefy	**recapitchulashun**	recapitulation
rascul	rascal	**recapitlate**	recapitulate
rashal	racial	**receed**	*recede, reseed*
rasheo	ratio	**receet**	*receipt, reseat*
rashun	ration	**receive**	receive
rashunal	*rational*	**receivible**	receivable
rashunale	*rationale*	**rech**	*retch, wretch*
ratchit	ratchet	**rechwazit**	requisite
rath	*wraith, wrath*	**reciept**	*receipt, reseat*
raucus	raucous	**recievable**	receivable
ravaj	*ravage*	**reciprocle**	reciprocal
ravanus	ravenous	**reck**	wreck
raveole	ravioli	**reckage**	wreckage
ravysh	*ravish*	**recognasance**	recognizance
rawt	*rot, wrought*	**recognise**	recognize
ray*	*re*	**recomend**	recommend
rayd	*raid, rayed*	**recomending**	recommending
rayn	*rain, reign, rein*	**reconasance**	reconnaissance
raysomay	résumé	**reconsiliashun**	reconciliation

WRONG	RIGHT	WRONG	RIGHT
reconvay	reconvey	reflekshun	reflection
reconveen	reconvene	refleksive	reflexive
recoop	recoup	reflex*	*reflects*
recooperate	recuperate	refoogee	refugee
recooperation	recuperation	refooj	refuge
recorse	recourse	refoose	refuse
recreashun	recreation	refrakshun	refraction
recroot	recruit	refrijerate	refrigerate
rectafy	rectify	refrijeration	refrigeration
recurent	recurrent	refusel	refusal
red*	*read*	refuss	refuse
redish	*radish, reddish*	refuzal	refusal
redoos	reduce	refyooj	refuge
reducshun	reduction	regamen	*regimen*
redundent	redundant	regament	*regiment*
redusable	reducible	regerjatashun	regurgitation
reeality	*reality, realty*	regreshun	regression
reebait	*rebait, rebate*	regretable	regrettable
reed*	*read*	regretably	*regrettably*
reek*	*wreak*	regrettfully	*regretfully*
reelayed	*relaid, relayed*	reguard	regard
reeltor	realtor	reguardless	regardless
reelty	*realty*	regulashun	regulation
reem	ream	regurjatation	regurgitation
reeth	*wreath, wreathe*	rehabilatate	rehabilitate
referance	*reference, referents*	rehersal	rehearsal
refered	referred	reiene	*rain, reign, rein*
referince	*reference*	rejament	*regiment*
referrents	*referents*	rejeem	*regime*
refewt	refute	rejenerate	regenerate
refewtable	refutable	rejeneration	regeneration
refiree	referee	rejestry	registry
reflecs	*reflects, reflex*	rejinsy	regency

The asterisk (*) next to boldface words flags "misspellings" that are also real words. For words that appear in italics, see Part II, "Sound-Alikes and Confusibles," to confirm your word choice.

WRONG	RIGHT	WRONG	RIGHT
rejister	*register*	relijon	religion
rejistrar	*registrar*	relijus	religious
rejistration	registration	relik	*relic*
rejun	region	relikt	*relict*
rejuvinate	rejuvenate	relingwish	relinquish
rek	*reck, wreck*	relm	realm
rekapitchulation	recapitulation	reluctence	reluctance
reker	recur	remady	remedy
rekering	recurring	remanant	remnant
rekomend	recommend	remanisance	reminiscence
rekon	reckon	Rembrant	Rembrandt
rekonasence	reconnaissance	remeedyal	remedial
rekonsignment	reconsignment	rememberance	remembrance
rekonsil	reconcile	remenisence	reminiscence
rekrut	recruit	reminise	reminisce
rekumbant	recumbent	remis	remiss
rekwasit	requisite	remitance	remittance
rekwasition	requisition	remmis	remiss
relacks	relax	remnent	remnant
relashunal	relational	remunarashun	remuneration
relatif	*relative*	ren	wren
relayd	*relaid, relayed*	renagade	*renegade*
rele	*real, reel*	renasance	renaissance
releef	relief	rench	wrench
releese	release	rendayvous	rendezvous
relegait	relegate	renforce	reinforce
releive	relieve	renig	*renege*
relevence	relevance	renouned	renowned
relevency	relevancy	renunseashun	renunciation
relevent	*relevant*	Reo Grand	Rio Grande
relgate	relegate	reostat	rheostat
reliabul	reliable	reparashun	reparation
relience	reliance	repatishun	repetition
religous	religious	repatishus	repetitious

WRONG	RIGHT	WRONG	RIGHT
repatwore	repertoire	resel	wrestle
repeel	*repeal*	resemblence	resemblance
repelent	repellent	resent*	*recent*
repell	*repel*	resepshun	reception
repentent	repentant	reseptacle	receptacle
repetishus	repetitious	reseptionist	receptionist
repewdiate	repudiate	reseptive	receptive
replaca	replica	reseptor	receptor
replacable	replaceable	reserrection	resurrection
replakashun	replication	reservor	reservoir
repleet	replete	resesses	recesses
reposatory	repository	resete	*receipt, reseat*
reprahensable	reprehensible	resheem	*regime*
repramand	reprimand	resical	recycle
repreeve	reprieve	residense	*residence, residents*
reprehensable	reprehensible	residjuel	residual
representitive	representative	resind	rescind
reprizal	reprisal	resipee	recipe
reprize	reprise	resipracate	reciprocate
reproch	reproach	resiprocal	reciprocal
repugnence	repugnance	resirjense	resurgence
repugnent	repugnant	resirvwar	reservoir
requesition	requisition	resistable	resistible
resadency	*residency*	resistence	resistance
resadents	*residence, residents*	resistent	resistant
resado	residue	resital	recital
resaleable	resalable	resonable	reasonable
resanater	resonator	resonent	resonant
resatation	recitation	respectfuly	*respectfully*
resead	*recede, reseed*	respectivly	*respectively*
reseet	*receipt, reseat*	respecttabl	*respectably*
reseeve	receive	resperater	respirator
reseevership	receivership	resperation	respiration

The asterisk (*) next to boldface words flags "misspellings" that are also real words. For words that appear in italics, see Part II, "Sound-Alikes and Confusibles," to confirm your word choice.

WRONG	RIGHT
respirater	respirator
respledant	resplendent
respondsively	*responsively*
responsability	responsibility
responsably	*responsibly*
ressle	wrestle
rest*	*wrest*
restatushun	restitution
restaurantur	restauranteur or restaurateur
restaurent	restaurant
restle	wrestle
restling	wrestling
restrane	restrain
restranet	restraint
restrant	restaurant
restrikshun	restriction
resumay	résumé
resurjence	resurgence
resusatation	resuscitation
resusatator	resuscitator
resusitate	resuscitate
retabushun	retribution
retaleate	retaliate
retanew	retinue
retardent	retardant
retasence	reticence
retched	wretched
retenshun	retention
retisence	reticence
retna	retina
retoric	rhetoric
retorical	rhetorical
retreeve	retrieve

WRONG	RIGHT
retreevel	retrieval
rettroactive	retroactive
reumatic	rheumatic
reumy	*rheumy, roomy*
revanew	revenue
reveer	revere
revelli	reveille
reverand	*reverend*
reverant	*reverent*
reversable	reversible
revew	*review, revue*
revishun	revision
revokable	revocable
revolushun	revolution
revoo	*review, revue*
rexamine	reexamine
reyl	*real, reel*
reyn	*reign, rein, rain*
reyoonyon	reunion
rezado	residue
rezamay	résumé
rezarect	resurrect
rezentment	resentment
rezidense	*residence, residents*
rezilyence	resilience
rezilyent	resilient
rezist	resist
rezistant	resistant
rezistence	resistance
rezolushun	resolution
rezolute	resolute
rezolution	resolution
rezolve	resolve
rezonable	reasonable

WRONG	RIGHT	WRONG	RIGHT
rezonance	resonance	rinkle	wrinkle
rezonant	resonant	rinoceros	rhinoceros
rezonate	resonate	riskay	*risque*
rezonater	resonator	riskey	*risky*
rezoom	resume	rist	wrist
rezort	resort	rite*	*right, wright, write*
rezult	result	ritechus	righteous
rhime	*rhyme, rime*	rithe	writhe
ri	*rye, wry*	rithim	rhythm
richual	ritual	rithmick	rhythmic
richusly	righteously	rittz	*ritz, writs*
ridacul	ridicule	rivit	rivet
ridance	riddance	rize	rise
ridiculus	ridiculous	rizen	risen
ridled	riddled	rizible	risible
riegn	*rain, reign, rein*	roat	*rote, wrote*
rifel	rifle	roccoco	rococo
rigamarole	rigmarole	roch	roach
riged	*ridged, rigid*	rodadendron	rhododendron
riger	*rigger, rigor*	Rode Island	Rhode Island
rigerus	rigorous	rode*	*road*
riggle	wriggle	Rodesha	Rhodesia
riggor	*rigger, rigor*	rododendron	rhododendron
right*	*rite, wright, write*	roed	*road, rode*
rightus	righteous	roes*	*rose, rows*
rigorus	rigorous	rog	rogue
rij	ridge	roll*	*role*
rijid	*rigid*	rondayvoo	rendezvous
rikoshay	ricochet	rong	wrong
rime*	*rhyme*	roo	*roux, rue*
rineosferus	rhinoceros	roobarb	rhubarb
rinestone	rhinestone	roobella	rubella
ring*	*wring*	rood*	*rude, rued*

The asterisk (*) next to boldface words flags "misspellings" that are also real words. For words that appear in italics, see Part II, "Sound-Alikes and Confusibles," to confirm your word choice.

WRONG	RIGHT
rooful	rueful
rooin	ruin
rooj	rouge
rool	rule
roolet	roulette
roomate	roommate
roomatic	rheumatic
roomatism	rheumatism
roomie	*roomy, rheumy*
roommer	*roomer, rumor*
root*	*route*
rooz	ruse
ros	*roes, rose, rows*
rot*	*wrought*
rote*	*wrote*
rotissirie	rotisserie
Rotwiler	Rottweiler
rouf	*rough, ruff*
rought	*rot, wrought*
rouz	rouse
rowd	*road, rode, rowed*
rowt	*rout, route*
roz	*roes, rose, rows*
rozin	rosin
rozy	rosy
rubarb	rhubarb
rubela	rubella
rudament	rudiment
rudamental	rudimental
rue*	*roux*
ruf	*rough, ruff*
rumbul	rumble
rumore	*roomer, rumor*
rung*	*wrung*

WRONG	RIGHT
rupchur	rupture
Rusha	Russia
rybald	ribald
ryeth	writhe
ryme	*rhyme, rime*
rythmic	rhythmic
rythum	rhythm

S

WRONG	RIGHT
sabataj	sabotage
sabatical	sabbatical
sabatur	saboteur
sabbeth	Sabbath
sachel	satchel
sachurate	saturate
sacket	socket
sackz	*sacks, sacs, sax*
sacome	succumb
sacrafice	sacrifice
sacrafishal	sacrificial
sacreligious	sacrilegious
sacretion	secretion
sacrosink	sacrosanct
sadan	sedan
sadate	sedate
Sadurday	Saturday
saef	safe
safire	sapphire
saflower	safflower
safron	saffron
safty	safety
sailyent	salient

WRONG	RIGHT	WRONG	RIGHT
sain	*sane, sein*	sangwine	sanguine
Sajatarius	Sagittarius	sanility	senility
sakarine	saccharine	sankchewary	sanctuary
Sakramento	Sacramento	sankshun	sanction
sakroskink	sacrosanct	sanwich	sandwich
saks	*sacs, sacks, sax*	sanzerif	sans serif
salava	saliva	sapeena	subpoena
salavary	salivary	saphire	sapphire
saleable	salable	sapose	suppose
saleen	saline	saprano	soprano
saleyent	salient	sapreem	supreme
salid	salad	sapress	suppress
salle	*sale, sail*	sar	czar or tsar
salm	psalm	sararity	sorority
salman	salmon	sarenity	serenity
salonn	*salon*	sarinj	syringe
saloot	salute	sarjent	sergeant
salow	*sallow*	sarkasm	sarcasm
salry	salary	sarkastic	sarcastic
salum	solemn	sasafras	sassafras
salune	*saloon*	Sascachawon	Saskatchewan
salution	solution	sashable	satiable
salvaj	*salvage*	sasheate	satiate
sametrical	symmetrical	sasparilla	sarsaparilla
samon	salmon	sasy	*sassy*
samwich	sandwich	satarise	satirize
San Deigo	San Diego	satastishen	statistician
San Fransisco	San Francisco	satearacal	satirical
San Hozay	San Jose	Saterday	Saturday
San Wan	San Juan	satilite	satellite
sanata	sonata	satir	*satire, satyr*
sanatarium	sanitarium	satiracal	satirical
sanatary	sanitary	satisfacsion	satisfaction

The asterisk (*) next to boldface words flags "misspellings" that are also real words. For words that appear in italics, see Part II, "Sound-Alikes and Confusibles," to confirm your word choice.

WRONG	RIGHT	WRONG	RIGHT
satisfing	satisfying	scimp	*skimp*
satyre	*satire, satyr*	scisors	scissors
sauft	soft	scoch	*Scotch*
sause	sauce	scolarly	scholarly
saut	sought	scorpeon	scorpion
sautay	sauté	scrip*	*script*
sav	salve	scrole	scroll
savana	savanna or savannah	scruntinise	scrutinize
savery	savory	scul	*scull, skull*
savir	*saver, savor*	sealous	zealous
savwafaire	savoir-faire	sean	*scene, seen*
savy	savvy	seas*	*cease, sees, seize*
savyour	*savior*	Sebaschean	Sebastian
sawsaj	sausage	seceed	secede
sawsy	*saucy*	seck	*sic, sick*
sax*	*sacs, sacks*	secracy	secrecy
saxaphone	saxophone	secretery	secretary
sayl	*sail, sale*	secureties	securities
sayleince	salience	sedament	sediment
sayve	save	sedashun	sedation
Sazarean	Caesarean	sede	*cede, seed*
scaberd	scabbard	seder	cedar
scafold	scaffold	sedintary	sedentary
Scandanavia	Scandinavia	sedishun	sedition
scaner	scanner	sedoos	seduce
scarsity	scarcity	see*	*sea*
scavenjer	scavenger	seecreet	*secrete*
scedule	schedule	seecret	*secret*
sceen	*scene, seen*	seecure	secure
scematic	schematic	seej	siege
sceme	scheme	seekwel	sequel
scenry	scenery	seeling	*ceiling, sealing*
sceptic	skeptic	seem*	*seam*
scewer	skewer	seement	cement

WRONG	RIGHT
seenile	senile
seenyer	senior
seeqwins	sequence, sequins
seer*	sear, sere
seerees	series
seerial	cereal, serial
seerra	sierra
seeryus	serious
seese	cease, seas, sees, seize
seesure	seizure
seeth	seethe
seev	sieve
seez	cease, seas, sees, seize
seezon	season
segragate	segregate
seige	siege
sein	sane, seine
seive	sieve
sekresy	secrecy
sekter	sector
sekular	secular
sekure	secure
sekwel	sequel
sekwens	sequence, sequins
sekwenshal	sequential
sekwester	sequester
selabate	celibate
selar	cellar, seller
selary	celery
selebration	celebration
selebrity	celebrity
seler	seller, cellar
seleschal	celestial

WRONG	RIGHT
self-sentered	self-centered
sell*	cell
sellaphane	cellophane
sellar	cellar, seller
sellular	cellular
selvaj	salvage, selvage
semacircle	semicircle
sematery	cemetery
sematrical	symmetrical
semblence	semblance
senareo	scenario
sences	census, senses
sene	scene, seen
senic	scenic
sensability	sensibility
sensabul	sensible
sense*	cents, scents
senser	censer, censor, sensor
senshul	sensual
sensor	censor, censor
sensored	censored
sensure	censure
sensus	census, senses
sentagrade	centigrade
sentament	sentiment
sentamental	sentimental
sentance	sentence
sentenyal	centennial
senter	center
sentimeter	centimeter
sentnal	sentinel
sentrifooj	centrifuge
sents	cents, scents, sense

The asterisk (*) next to boldface words flags "misspellings" that are also real words. For words that appear in italics, see Part II, "Sound-Alikes and Confusibles," to confirm your word choice.

WRONG	RIGHT	WRONG	RIGHT
senyor	senior	servive	survive
seperate	separate	Sesarean	Caesarean
seperately	separately	seseat	deceit
seperation	separation	sesede	secede
seprano	soprano	seshure	seizure
septer	scepter	sesion	*cession, session*
seqwence	*sequence, sequins*	sessame	sesame
seramic	ceramic	settel	settle
seramonial	ceremonial	seudonym	pseudonym
seranade	serenade	seventyeth	seventieth
serch	search	severel	several
sercharge	surcharge	severence	severance
sercophagus	sarcophagus	sevinteen	seventeen
sercut	circuit	sew*	*so, sow*
sere*	*sear, seer*	sex*	*sects*
sereous	*serious, serous*	sfearacal	spherical
sergent	sergeant	sfeer	sphere
serj	*serge, surge*	sfinkter	sphincter
sermize	surmise	sfinx	sphinx
serogate	surrogate	shaam	*sham, shame*
serplis	*surplice, surplus*	shado	shadow
serprize	surprise	shagrin	chagrin
serrebral	cerebral	shagrinned	chagrined
serrender	surrender	shagy	shaggy
serround	surround	shaid	shade
serrum	serum	shaik	*shake, sheik*
sertain	certain	shaim	*shame*
sertax	surtax	shakle	shackle
sertificate	certificate	shalay	chalet
sertin	certain	shalome	shalom
servatude	servitude	shalow	*shallow*
servay	survey	shambul	shamble
servex	cervix	shampane	champagne
servicable	serviceable	shandaleer	chandelier

WRONG	RIGHT	WRONG	RIGHT
Shanghi	Shanghai	**shrapnal**	shrapnel
shaperon	chaperon or chaperone	**shreek**	shriek
sharaid	charade	**shrival**	shrivel
sharlatan	charlatan	**shrood**	shrewd
shaw	shawl	**shuder**	*shudder*
sheat	*sheet*	**shugar**	sugar
sheatheing	sheathing	**shugarie**	sugary
sheef	*sheaf*	**shur**	sure
sheek	*chic, sheik*	**shurely**	*surely*
sheeth	*sheath*	**shurest**	surest
sheild	shield	**shus**	shoes
sheir	*shear, sheer*	**shute**	*chute, shoot*
sheperd	shepherd	**shuter**	*shutter*
sherbert	sherbet	**shuttel**	shuttle
shere	*shear, sheer*	**shuv**	shove
sherk	shirk	**Shyanne**	Cheyenne
sherrif	sheriff	**sianide**	cyanide
shething	sheathing	**sibernetics**	cybernetics
shic	*chic, sheik*	**siberspace**	cyberspace
shikanery	chicanery	**sicadelic**	psychedelic
shinning	shining	**sickamor**	sycamore
shirbert	sherbet	**sid**	*side, sighed*
shirly	*surely*	**sidishus**	seditious
shivalrus	chivalrous	**sien**	*scion, sign, sine, syne*
shlock	schlock	**siense**	science
shoan	*shone, shown*	**sientific**	scientific
shofur	chauffeur	**sieshur**	seizure
shol	shoal	**siesmograph**	seismograph
sholder	shoulder	**sieze**	*cease, seas, sees, seize*
shoo*	*shoe*	**siezing**	seizing
shorteand	*shortened, shorthand*	**siezure**	seizure
showen	*shone, shown*	**sifon**	siphon
showvinism	chauvinism	**sighth**	scythe

The asterisk (*) next to boldface words flags "misspellings" that are also real words. For words that appear in italics, see Part II, "Sound-Alikes and Confusibles," to confirm your word choice.

WRONG	RIGHT
significence	significance
significent	significant
sihed	*side, sighed*
sihs	*sighs, size*
sik	*sic, sick*
sikada	cicada
sikiatric	psychiatric
sikiatrist	psychiatrist
sikiatry	psychiatry
sikick	*psychic*
siklone	cyclone
siklotron	cyclotron
sikologickle	psychological
sikologist	psychologist
sikology	psychology
sikometric	psychometric
sikosis	psychosis
sikul	cycle
silable	syllable
silacon	*silicon, silicone*
silant	silent
silender	cylinder
silense	silence
silhoette	silhouette
silinder	cylinder
sillabul	syllable
sillabus	syllabus
sillacon	*silicon, silicone*
sillowette	silhouette
simalarity	similarity
simalated	simulated
simaler	similar
simbal	*cymbal, symbol*
Simese	Siamese

WRONG	RIGHT
simetrical	symmetrical
simfony	symphony
simillitude	similitude
simmatry	symmetry
simpathize	sympathize
simpathy	sympathy
simplafying	simplifying
simpozeum	symposium
simptomatic	symptomatic
simtom	symptom
simultaneus	simultaneous
simultanity	simultaneity
simultanous	simultaneous
simyoulate	simulate
sinacal	cynical
sinagog	synagogue or synagog
sinakal	cynical
sinama	cinema
sinamon	cinnamon
sinaster	sinister
sinc	*sink, sync*
sincerly	sincerely
sindacate	syndicate
sindrome	syndrome
sine*	*scion, sign, syne*
sinerje	synergy
sinester	sinister
singuler	singular
sinide	cyanide
sinj	singe
sinkronize	synchronize
sinkronus	synchronous
sinonamous	synonymous
sinonym	synonym

WRONG	RIGHT	WRONG	RIGHT
sinopsis	synopsis	sirpent	serpent
sinous	*sinuous*	sirplus	*surplice, surplus*
sinse	since	sirprize	surprise
sinseer	sincere	sirrealism	surrealism
sinseerly	sincerely	sirrender	surrender
sinseraty	sincerity	sirriptitious	surreptitious
Sinsinati	Cincinnati	sirrogate	surrogate
sintax	syntax	sirrosis	cirrhosis
sinthases	synthesis	sirrus	*cirrous, cirrus, serous*
sinthesize	synthesize	sirtax	surtax
sinthetic	synthetic	sirup	syrup
sinyews	*sinews*	sirvacal	cervical
sinyoous	*sinuous*	sirvay	survey
siphilis	syphilis	sirvaylence	surveillance
sipress	cypress	sirvival	survival
sircharge	surcharge	sissors	scissors
sirculation	circulation	sist	cyst
sircumflex	circumflex	sistamatic	systematic
sircumfrence	circumference	sistern	cistern
sircumscribe	circumscribe	sistim	system
sircumspection	circumspection	sitadel	citadel
sircumstance	circumstance	sitashun	citation
sireen	siren	sitawashun	situation
sirf	*serf, surf*	sitazen	citizen
sirface	surface	sith	scythe
sirfit	surfeit	situwate	situate
siringe	syringe	siv	sieve
sirjacal	surgical	sivic	civic
sirjons	surgeons	sivil	civil
sirket	circuit	sivilize	civilize
sirkling	circling	sixtyeth	sixtieth
sirly	*surly*	siz	*sighs, size*
sirname	surname	sizemograph	seismograph

The asterisk (*) next to boldface words flags "misspellings" that are also real words. For words that appear in italics, see Part II, "Sound-Alikes and Confusibles," to confirm your word choice.

WRONG	RIGHT	WRONG	RIGHT
sizors	scissors	skitish	skittish
skabard	scabbard	skitzophrenia	schizophrenia
skafold	scaffold	skoch	Scotch
skalastic	scholastic	skof	scoff
skald	scald	skolar	scholar
skale	scale	skolarship	scholarship
skalewag	scallywag	skolastic	scholastic
skallion	scallion	skolded	scolded
skalp	scalp	skons	sconce
skalpel	scalpel	skool	school
skam	*scam*	skooner	schooner
skamper	scamper	skoop	scoop
skan	*scan*	skooter	scooter
skandalus	scandalous	skope	scope
Skandinavia	Scandinavia	skorch	scorch
skanner	scanner	skorj	scourge
skapegoat	scapegoat	skorn	scorn
skar	scar	skorpion	scorpion
skarsity	scarcity	skoundral	scoundrel
skathing	scathing	skout	scout
skatter	scatter	skow	scowl
skavenjer	scavenger	skram	scram
skech	sketch	skrawny	scrawny
skedjewel	schedule	skreem	scream
skeduling	scheduling	skreen	screen
skeeme	scheme	skrimp	*scrimp*
skelaton	skeleton	skrip	*scrip, script*
skeptick	skeptic	skroll	scroll
skeptisism	skepticism	skroo	screw
skermish	skirmish	skrounj	scrounge
skien	skein	skrub	scrub
skilfull	skillful	skrumpshus	scrumptious
sking	skiing	skrunch	scrunch
skism	schism	skrupul	scruple

WRONG	RIGHT	WRONG	RIGHT
skrupulous	scrupulous	skyskraper	skyscraper
skrutinize	scrutinize	slae	*slay, sleigh*
skrutiny	scrutiny	slawter	slaughter
skuba	scuba	sleepaly	sleepily
skuf	scuff	sleeze	sleaze
skul	*scull, skull*	slege	sledge
skulpchur	*sculpture*	sleih	*slay, sleigh*
skulptor	*sculptor*	slieght	*sleight, slight*
skum	scum	sliker	slicker
skurry	scurry	slippry	slippery
skurvy	scurvy	slising	slicing
skutle	scuttle	slite	*sleight, slight*
skuttelbut	scuttlebutt	slitly	slightly
skuwer	skewer	slo	*sloe, slow*
skwad	squad	slogen	slogan
skwalk	squawk	sloo	*slew, slough*
skwall	squall	slooth	sleuth
skware	square	sluf	*slough*
skwash	squash	slufed	sloughed
skwat	squat	slugard	sluggard
skweek	squeak	sluge	sludge
skweemish	squeamish	slugish	sluggish
skweeze	squeeze	sluse	sluice
skwelch	squelch	slyte	*sleight, slight*
skwerl	squirrel	smethereens	smithereens
skwert	squirt	smootch	smooch
skwid	squid	smoth	smooth
skwint	squint	smugling	smuggling
skwire	squire	smuther	smother
skwirm	squirm	snach	snatch
skwirrul	squirrel	snair	snare
skwish	squish	snauzer	schnauzer
skying	skiing	sneek	sneak

The asterisk (*) next to boldface words flags "misspellings" that are also real words. For words that appear in italics, see Part II, "Sound-Alikes and Confusibles," to confirm your word choice.

WRONG	RIGHT	WRONG	RIGHT
snevils	snivels	Solaman	Solomon
snich	snitch	solanoid	solenoid
sniep	snipe	solatear	solitaire
snif	sniff	solatude	solitude
sniful	sniffle	sole*	*soul*
snivul	snivel	solem	solemn
snor	snore	soler	solar
snorkle	snorkel	solilokwe	soliloquy
snoty	snotty	solis	solace
snuf	snuff	solisator	solicitor
snuggel	snuggle	solisitus	solicitous
snugling	snuggling	solitair	solitaire
so*	*sew, sow*	soljer	soldier
soal	*sole, soul*	soll	*sole, soul*
soape	soapy	solld	*sold, soled*
soar*	*sore*	solliloguy	soliloquy
sobriaty	sobriety	solumn	solemn
sociaty	society	solushun	solution
sockit	socket	solvansy	solvency
Socratease	Socrates	som	*some, sum*
soden	sodden	sombraro	sombrero
sodeum	sodium	somersalt	somersault
soek	*soak, soke*	someware	somewhere
soer	*sewer, suer*	somnalence	somnolence
sofisticate	sophisticate	Sonday	Sunday
sofistry	sophistry	sonet	sonnet
sofmore	sophomore	sonnata	sonata
Sofoclez	Sophocles	soo	sue
sojurn	sojourn	sooage	*sewage*
sojurnor	sojourner	soodonim	pseudonym
soke*	*soak*	soodosience	pseudoscience
soker	soccer	sooer	*sewer, suer*
soket	socket	sooerage	*sewerage*
soladarity	solidarity	sooflay	soufflé

WRONG	RIGHT	WRONG	RIGHT
soop	soup	sovarin	sovereign
sooper	*super*	sovrenty	sovereignty
soopine	supine	sovyet	Soviet
soor	*sewer, suer*	sowth	south
soot	*suit*	spachula	spatula
soovanir	souvenir	spagetti	spaghetti
sope	soap	spaid	*spade, spayed*
sophestry	sophistry	Spanesh	Spanish
sophmore	sophomore	spanyel	spaniel
sor	*soar, sore*	sparadic	sporadic
Sorbon	Sorbonne	sparce	sparse
sorceror	sorcerer	sparkaler	sparkler
sord	*soared, sword*	sparkel	sparkle
sorgum	sorghum	sparow	sparrow
soriasis	psoriasis	spashall	spatial
sorid	sordid	spashus	*spacious*
sorley	sorely	spastisity	spasticity
sorrority	sorority	spatil	spatial
sorsary	sorcery	spaun	spawn
sorse	source	spayd	*spade, spayed*
sorserer	sorcerer	spazmodic	spasmodic
sory	*soiree, sorry*	speach	speech
soshabul	sociable	spearit	spirit
soshal	social	specal	special
soshally	socially	specificly	specifically
sosiety	society	speciman	specimen
sotay	sauté	specktrum	spectrum
sothe	*soothe*	spectacul	spectacle
sourkraut	sauerkraut	spectater	spectator
South Dacota	South Dakota	spector	specter
South Karalina		spedometer	speedometer
	South Carolina	speedaly	speedily
Soux	Sioux	speek	speak

The asterisk (*) next to boldface words flags "misspellings" that are also real words. For words that appear in italics, see Part II, "Sound-Alikes and Confusibles," to confirm your word choice.

WRONG	RIGHT	WRONG	RIGHT
speeshus	*specious*	spontanous	spontaneous
spegetti	spaghetti	spoonfulls	spoonfuls
spektacal	spectacle	spowse	spouse
spekulate	speculate	spralled	sprawled
sper	spur	spratic	sporadic
sperious	spurious	sprauled	sprawled
spert	spurt	spred	spread
spesamen	specimen	spredshet	spreadsheet
speshal	special	sprinkul	sprinkle
speshalist	specialist	spritely	sprightly
speshees	*species*	sproket	sprocket
speshus	*specious*	sproos	spruce
spesiman	specimen	sprowt	sprout
sphingks	sphinx	spureus	spurious
sphinkter	sphincter	squegee	squeegee
spickit	spigot	squeltch	squelch
spie	spy	squirel	squirrel
spindul	spindle	squot	squat
spiney	spiny	stabalize	stabilize
spinich	spinach	stachew	*statue*
spirachual	spiritual	stachur	*stature*
spirt	spurt	stachute	*statute*
spital	spittle	stade	*staid, stayed*
spitefull	spiteful	stadeum	stadium
spitle	spittle	staek	*stake, steak*
splended	splendid	staer	*stair, stare*
splender	splendor	staf	*staff*
sploch	splotch	stager	stagger
splocht	splotched	stagnashun	stagnation
spoling	spooling	stagnent	stagnant
sponj	sponge	stail	stale
sponjee	spongy	staj	stage
sponser	sponsor	stak	stack
spontanayaty	spontaneity	stakato	staccato

WRONG	RIGHT	WRONG	RIGHT
stalagmit	*stalagmite*	**stedy**	steady
stalagtite	*stalactite*	**steepul**	steeple
stallwart	stalwart	**steller**	stellar
stalyon	stallion	**stelth**	stealth
stamena	stamina	**stelthy**	stealthy
stampeed	stampede	**stensil**	stencil
stanchon	stanchion	**step***	*steppe*
standerd	standard	**sterule**	sterile
stane	stain	**steryotype**	stereotype
stansa	stanza	**stethascope**	stethoscope
staplar	stapler	**stevadoor**	stevedore
stare*	*stair*	**stewerdess**	stewardess
starewell	stairwell	**stich**	stitch
startuling	startling	**stie**	sty
stary	starry	**stifening**	stiffening
stashunary	*stationary, stationery*	**stigmatise**	stigmatize
		stigme	stigma
statatishan	statistician	**stikler**	stickler
stationery*	*stationary*	**stile***	*style*
statis	status	**stilletto**	stiletto
statment	statement	**stilus**	stylus
stattistics	statistics	**stime**	stymie
stattute	*statute*	**stimulent**	stimulant
statuetory	statutory	**stine**	stein
status kwo	status quo	**stipand**	stipend
stawart	stalwart	**stipulashun**	stipulation
stayd	*staid, stayed*	**stirup**	stirrup
stayk	*stake, steak*	**stoasism**	stoicism
steal*	*steel*	**stockaid**	stockade
stearage	steerage	**stoe**	stow
sted	stead	**stogee**	stogie
stedaly	steadily	**stoick**	stoic
stedfast	steadfast	**stojee**	stodgy

The asterisk (*) next to boldface words flags "misspellings" that are also real words. For words that appear in italics, see Part II, "Sound-Alikes and Confusibles," to confirm your word choice.

WRONG	RIGHT
stomek	stomach
stooardess	stewardess
stoped	stopped
stoping	stopping
stradling	straddling
straggul	straggle
stragling	straggling
strait*	*straight*
straiten*	*straighten*
strangalation	strangulation
strangul	strangle
stratagee	strategy
strate	*straight, strait*
strateagic	strategic
stratijim	strategem
stratim	stratum
strattejy	strategy
strayt	*straight, strait*
strayten	*straighten, straiten*
strech	stretch
strecher	stretcher
streek	streak
strenth	strength
strenthen	strengthen
strenueus	strenuous
strewzel	streusel
strickchur	*stricture*
stricknine	strychnine
stricly	strictly
striken	stricken
strikout	strikeout
strinjent	stringent
striped*	*stripped*
stroginoff	stroganoff

WRONG	RIGHT
struckchur	*structure*
studeing	studying
studeus	studious
stumach	stomach
stupendus	stupendous
stupidaty	stupidity
stupify	stupefy
stupoor	stupor
styme	stymie
stymulate	*stimulate*
styreen	styrene
suasidal	suicidal
sub-committee	subcommittee
subdew	subdue
subdood	subdued
subdrectory	subdirectory
subjagate	subjugate
sublimanal	subliminal
submershun	submersion
submirsable	submersible
submirshun	submersion
submisive	submissive
submited	submitted
subordanate	subordinate
subpeena	subpoena
subsadize	subsidize
subsady	subsidy
subscrip	subscript
subserveence	subservience
subsideary	subsidiary
subsistance	subsistence
substanshal	substantial
substatushun	substitution
substence	substance

WRONG	RIGHT	WRONG	RIGHT
subtrafuge	subterfuge	sullin	sullen
sucatash	succotash	sulten	sultan
suceed	succeed	sultrey	sultry
sucessful	successful	sum*	*some*
sucession	succession	sumary/sumery	*summary,*
sucessive	successive		*summery*
sucksessor	successor	sumbrero	sombrero
suckshun	suction	sumed	summed
suckulant	succulent	sumer	summer
sucome	succumb	sumit	summit
sucor	*succor, sucker*	summarise	summarize
sucsessor	successor	sumon	summon
sucshun	suction	sumoned	*summoned*
sudonim	pseudonym	sun*	*son*
sueaside	suicide	sunbern	sunburn
sueper	super	sundile	sundial
sufering	suffering	sundrey	sundry
sufficent	sufficient	sunkin	sunken
suffishently	sufficiently	supeena	subpoena
sufice	suffice	supeened	subpoenaed
sufix	suffix	superceed	supersede
suflay	soufflé	superfishal	superficial
sufraj	suffrage	superflueus	superfluous
sufuse	suffuse	superintendant	superintendent
sugjest	suggest	superscrip	superscript
sugjestable	suggestible	superseed	supersede
sugjestion	suggestion	supersileus	supercillious
sugjestive	suggestive	superstishus	superstitious
suker/sukor	*succor, sucker*	supervize	supervise
suksessful	successful	supervizor	supervisor
suksinct	succinct	supirb	superb
sulfide	sulphide	suplant	supplant
sulfir	sulfur	supose	suppose

The asterisk (*) next to boldface words flags "misspellings" that are also real words. For words that appear in italics, see Part II, "Sound-Alikes and Confusibles," to confirm your word choice.

WRONG	RIGHT
suppel	supple
supplament	supplement
supremesy	supremacy
supress	suppress
supressant	suppressant
suprise	surprise
supterfuge	subterfuge
suptle	subtle
supul	supple
sureal	surreal
surealism	surrealism
surf*	*serf*
surfit	surfeit
surj	*serge, surge*
surjacal	surgical
surjery	surgery
surjon	surgeon
surloin	sirloin
surmize	surmise
surpliz	*surplice, surplus*
surprize	surprise
surptishus	surreptitious
surtain	certain
surveilance	surveillance
surviveable	survivable
surviver	survivor
susceptable	susceptible
suspeck	suspect
suspendors	suspenders
suspeshun	suspicion
suspinshun	suspension
suspishus	suspicious
suspition	suspicion
susseptible	susceptible

WRONG	RIGHT
sustenence	sustenance
sutable	suitable
suthe	*soothe*
suthern	southern
suttle	subtle
suttler	subtler
suttlety	subtlety
suttly	subtly
suvanear	souvenir
swaath	*swath*
swach	*swatch*
swager	swagger
swaid	*suede, swayed*
sware	swear
swav	suave
swayth	*swathe*
sweetner	sweetener
swerl	swirl
swet	sweat
swete	*suite, sweet*
swich	switch
swiming	swimming
swindel	swindle
swirve	swerve
Switserland	Switzerland
syatica	sciatica
syfilis	syphilis
sykone	cyclone
sylable	syllable
sylabus	syllabus
symetrical	symmetrical
symfony	symphony
sympozeum	symposium
symtom	symptom

WRONG	RIGHT
synacal	cynical
synanym	synonym
synchronus	synchronous
syndacate	syndicate
synegog	synagog or synagogue
synerje	synergy
synerjetic	synergetic
synk	*sink, sync*
synkopashun	syncopation
synkronize	synchronize
synonim	synonym
synthasis	synthesis
synthesise	synthesize
synulate	simulate
syphillis	syphilis
systamatic	systematic
systemetically	systematically
systum	system
sythe	scythe

T

WRONG	RIGHT
tabacko	tobacco
taberacul	tabernacle
tablow	tableau
tabu	taboo
tabulaytor	tabulator
tackturn	taciturn
tafeta	taffeta
tai	*Thai, tie*
tailess	tailless
tailight	taillight

WRONG	RIGHT
tailsman	*talesman, talisman*
tair	*tare, tear*
tak	*tack, tact*
taked	*tacked, tact*
tako	taco
takometer	tachometer
taks	*tacks, tax*
takt	*tacked, tact*
taktishan	tactician
takturn	taciturn
takul	tackle
Talahasee	Tallahassee
Talame	Ptolemy
talant	talent
tale*	*tail*
talezman	*talesman, talisman*
Talmood	Talmud
talun	talon
tamally	tamale
tambareen	tambourine
tandum	tandem
tangul	tangle
tanjable	tangible
tanjalo	tangelo
tanjareen	tangerine
tanjenshal	tangential
tanjent	tangent
tanjible	tangible
tannalize	tantalize
tapology	topology
tappd	*taped, tapped*
tapyoka	tapioca
taranchula	tarantula

The asterisk (*) next to boldface words flags "misspellings" that are also real words. For words that appear in italics, see Part II, "Sound-Alikes and Confusibles," to confirm your word choice.

WRONG	RIGHT
tare*	*tear*
tarpolin	tarpaulin
tarriff	tariff
tarter	tartar
tasit	tacit
tassle	tassel
tasteing	tasting
tatatate	tête-à-tête
tatoo	tattoo
tattletail	tattletale
tauht	*taught, taut*
tautalojacal	tautological
taward	toward
tawpe	taupe
tawt	*taut, taught*
tax*	*tacks, tax*
taxible	taxable
taxing*	taxiing
tayl	*tail, tale*
taylor	tailor
tayped	*taped*
tayper/taypir	*taper, tapir*
Tazmanea	Tasmania
te	*tea, tee*
teadyum	tedium
teadyus	tedious
team*	*teem*
tearanny	tyranny
teariff	tariff
teatotaler	teetotaler
teaz	*teas, tease*
technulogy	technology
tecknacal	technical
tecknacality	technicality
teckneek	technic
tecknology	technology
tedeous	tedious
tee*	tea
teech	teach
teekeala	tequilla
teknacality	technicality
tekneek	technique
teknishan	technician
teknology	technology
tekstile	textile
Teksus	Texas
tektonic	tectonic
telacomunicashun	telecommunication
telafone	telephone
telagraph	telegraph
telavise	televise
Telnet	Telenet
telogram	telegram
teme	*team, teem*
temperary	temporary
temperment	temperament
temperture	temperature
tempestyus	tempestuous
templet	template
temporarly	temporarily
temporel	temporal
tempra	tempera
temprachur	temperature
temprament	temperament
temprance	temperance
tempul	temple
temt	tempt

WRONG	RIGHT	WRONG	RIGHT
temtation	temptation	**terrafy**	terrify
tenabul	tenable	**terrase**	terrace
tenacal	tentacle	**terreschial**	terrestrial
tenament	tenement	**terret**	turret
Tenasee	Tennessee	**terreyer**	terrier
tenashus	tenacious	**tersheary**	tertiary
tenasity	tenacity	**tertul**	turtle
tendancy	tendency	**testacal**	testicle
tenden	tendon	**testamony**	testimony
tenent	*tenant*	**tetnus**	tetanus
tener	*tenner, tenor*	**texchur**	texture
tenit	*tenet*	**thach**	thatch
tennor	*tenner, tenor*	**thare**	*their, there, they're*
tennus	*tenace, tennis*	**tharefore**	*therefor, therefore*
tentitive	tentative	**thawd**	thawed
tentz	*tense, tents*	**thawtful**	thoughtful
tenyur	*tenure*	**thayr**	*their, there*
tenze	*tense, tents*	**thayrs**	*there's, theirs*
terarium	terrarium	**the***	*thee*
terbin	*turban, turbine*	**thearetacal**	theoretical
terbojet	turbojet	**theatracal**	theatrical
terbulance	turbulence	**theatre***	theater
tere	*tear*	**theem**	theme
tereaki	teriyaki	**theery**	theory
terestrial	terrestrial	**theevary**	thievery
terf	turf	**thense**	thence
terkois	turquoise	**therapewtic**	therapeutic
termanology	terminology	**therefor***	*therefore*
terminel	terminal	**therize**	theorize
tern*	*turn*	**thermus**	thermos
ternkey	turnkey	**therteen**	thirteen
tero	tarot	**therum**	theorem
terodaktul	pterodactyl	**thery**	theory

The asterisk (*) next to boldface words flags "misspellings" that are also real words. For words that appear in italics, see Part II, "Sound-Alikes and Confusibles," to confirm your word choice.

WRONG	RIGHT
thesarus	thesaurus
thevish	thievish
thickning	thickening
thimbul	thimble
thime	*thyme*
thinest	thinnest
thirtyeth	thirtieth
thissle	thistle
thorasic	thoracic
thorney	thorny
thorogh	*thorough*
thot	thought
thousanth	thousandth
thousend	thousand
thrashe	*thrash*
thred	thread
threshhold	threshold
threten	threaten
thriftee	thrifty
thrish	*thresh*
thron	*throne, thrown*
thros	*throes, throws*
throte	throat
thru	*threw, through*
thruout	throughout
thuroe	*thorough*
Thurzday	Thursday
thwort	thwart
ti	*Thai, tie*
tickleing	tickling
ticoon	tycoon
tide*	*tied*
tidey	tidy
tiecoon	tycoon

WRONG	RIGHT
tiefoid	typhoid
tiek	tyke
tiep	type
tierant	tyrant
tierantacal	tyrannical
tierany	tyranny
tifoid	typhoid
tik	*tic, tick*
tike	tyke
tikul	tickle
til	till
tim	*thyme, time*
timbar/timbir	*timbre, timber*
timeing	timing
timerous	timorous
timpanee	tympany
tinee	tinny
tineness	tinniness
tingchur	tincture
tinsil	tinsel
tipacal	typical
tipe	type
tipefase	typeface
tipewriting	typewriting
tipler	tippler
tipography	*typography*
tiranize	tyrannize
tirban	*turban, turbine*
tirjid	*turgid*
tirkey	turkey
tirminal	terminal
tirmoil	turmoil
tirn	*tern, turn*
tirnip	turnip

WRONG	RIGHT	WRONG	RIGHT
tishoe	tissue	**toon**	tune
tittillate	titillate	**toonic**	tunic
to*	*too, two*	**toopay**	toupee
tobacko	tobacco	**Tootonic**	Teutonic
tode	*toad, toed, towed*	**tootor**	tutor
todler	toddler	**Toozday**	Tuesday
toe*	*tow*	**topacal**	topical
toepaz	topaz	**torchurous**	*torturous*
toepography	*topography*	**torent**	torrent
togethur	together	**tork**	torque
toilsom	toilsome	**tormenter**	tormentor
tok	*toke, toque*	**torpedoze**	torpedoes
tokin	token	**torrenshal**	torrential
toksic	toxic	**torshun**	torsion
told*	*tolled*	**tortealya**	tortilla
tolerent	tolerant	**tortewus**	*tortuous*
tolrable	tolerable	**tortus**	*tortoise*
tolrance	tolerance	**tortyus**	*tortious*
tomain	ptomaine	**Tosh Maha**	Taj Mahal
tommato	tomato	**totle**	total
tommorrow	tomorrow	**totled**	totaled
tomyhawk	tomahawk	**tourniment**	tournament
tonage	*tonnage*	**tournquet**	tourniquet
tonel	tonal	**toussle**	tousle
tonite	tonight	**towle**	towel
tonsallitis	tonsillitis	**towt**	tout
too*	*to, two*	**toxacology**	toxicology
toob	tube	**toylet**	toilet
tooberculosis	tuberculosis	**tracea**	trachea
tooishun	tuition	**tradishunal**	traditional
toom	tomb	**tragicaly**	tragically
toomor	tumor	**traid**	trade
toomstone	tombstone	**traitorus**	traitorous

The asterisk (*) next to boldface words flags "misspellings" that are also real words. For words that appear in italics, see Part II, "Sound-Alikes and Confusibles," to confirm your word choice.

WRONG	RIGHT	WRONG	RIGHT
trajady	tragedy	tranzlate	translate
trajic	tragic	tranzmit	transmit
trajically	tragically	tranzparant	transparent
trak	track, tract	tranzverse	*transverse*
trakshun	traction	tranzvestite	transvestite
traktabul	tractable	trapazoid	trapezoid
traktor	tractor	trapeas	trapeze
traleblazer	trailblazer	trate	trait
trampaleen	trampoline	trater	traitor
trampul	trample	traumatise	traumatize
transative	transitive	travale	travail
transatory	transitory	traviled	traveled
transeent	transient	travler	traveler
transend	transcend	travurse	*traverse*
transendence	transcendence	tray*	*trey*
transendental	transcendental	trea	trio
transferance	transference	treatis	*treaties, treatise*
transfered	transferred	trebutary	tributary
Transilvanea	Transylvania	trecherus	treacherous
transishun	transition	tred	tread
translater	translator	treemendus	tremendous
translusent	translucent	treetees	*treaties, treatise*
transmishun	transmission	trelis	trellis
transmital	transmittal	trembul	tremble
transmited	transmitted	tremmor	tremor
transmiter	transmitter	trepadashun	trepidation
transpoz	transpose	treshur	treasure
transum	transom	treshurer	treasurer
transvers	*transverse*	treshury	treasury
tranzetory	transitory	tressle	trestle
tranzgress	transgress	tribulasun	tribulation
tranzit	transit	triganometry	trigonometry
tranzition	transition	trikal	trickle
tranzlashun	translation	trilojee	trilogy

WRONG	RIGHT	WRONG	RIGHT
triming	trimming	trycycal	tricycle
trinaty	trinity	tryes	tries
tring	trying	tryful	trifle
tringket	trinket	trypod	tripod
triplacat	triplicate	tryumphant	triumphant
tripul	triple	tuberkulosis	tuberculosis
triseratops	triceratops	tuch	touch
trist	tryst	tucksedo	tuxedo
triumf	triumph	Tuewsday	Tuesday
triumfant	triumphant	tuf	tough
triveal	trivial	tuks	*tucks, tux*
trof	trough	tumbul	tumble
troley	trolley	tun*	*ton*
troop*	*troupe*	tung	tongue
trooth	truth	tunling	tunneling
trounse	trounce	tunnul	tunnel
trowzers	trousers	turbin	*turban, turbine*
trubadoor	troubadour	turbulance	turbulence
truckulant	truculent	turist	tourist
truely	truly	turkwoys	turquoise
truent	truant	turnaket	tourniquet
truging	trudging	turnament	tournament
truj	trudge	turpatude	turpitude
trunkate	truncate	turtul	turtle
trupe	*troop, troupe*	Tuson	Tucson
trused	*trussed, trust*	tutalaj	tutelage
truso	trousseau	tuter	tutor
trust*	*trussed*	tutoryal	tutorial
truste	*trustee, trusty*	tux*	*tucks*
tryangle	triangle	twelth	twelfth
tryangular	triangular	twentyeth	twentieth
trybal	tribal	twerl	twirl
tryco	tricot	twich	twitch

The asterisk (*) next to boldface words flags "misspellings" that are also real words. For words that appear in italics, see Part II, "Sound-Alikes and Confusibles," to confirm your word choice.

WRONG	RIGHT
twilite	twilight
tydy	tidy
tye	*Thai, tie*
tyer	*tear, tier*
tyfoid	typhoid
tyfoon	typhoon
tyme	*thyme, time*
typicle	typical
tyrade	tirade
tyranical	tyrannical
tyrranny	tyranny

U

WRONG	RIGHT
ubickwity	ubiquity
ubikwatus	ubiquitous
uew	*ewe, yew, you*
ufamizm	*euphemism*
uforia	euphoria
ugle	ugly
ujenic	eugenic
ukalayle	ukulele
ukaliptus	eucalyptus
uker	euchre
Uklid	Euclid
ulogee	euology
ulojize	eulogize
ulser	ulcer
ulserate	ulcerate
ulserus	ulcerous
ultamatum	ultimatum
ultearyor	ulterior
ultrasonik	ultrasonic

WRONG	RIGHT
ultravilet	ultraviolet
umbilicle	umbilical
umbrela	umbrella
umbrij	umbrage
unaficashun	unification
unafy	unify
unalateral	unilateral
unalienable	inalienable
unaltared	unaltered
unanmous	unanimous
unaversal	universal
uncany	uncanny
uncondishunal	unconditional
uncontrolably	uncontrollably
uncooth	uncouth
uncshus	unctuous
uncul	uncle
unculchurd	uncultured
undaunded	undaunted
underneth	underneath
underrite	underwrite
undoo	*undo, undue*
undoutedly	undoubtedly
undullate	undulate
unecessary	unnecessary
uneek	unique
unek	eunuch
unekseptionable	*unexceptionable*
unerth	unearth
unexseptional	*unexceptional*
unisen	unison
universaty	university
universel	universal

WRONG	RIGHT
unkemt	unkempt
unkjalate	undulate
unkshus	unctuous
unlawfull	unlawful
unmanagable	unmanageable
unmistakeable	unmistakable
unmitagated	unmitigated
unnecesary	unnecessary
unnesessaraly	unnecessarily
unnurve	unnerve
unpresedented	unprecedented
unreel*	*unreal*
unsekured	unsecured
unskrupulus	unscrupulous
unsolisited	unsolicited
untenabul	untenable
untill	until
unweeldy	unwieldy
unwonted*	*unwanted*
unyun	onion
upgraid	upgrade
upheavle	upheaval
upholsteror	upholsterer
uplode	upload
urbin	*urban*
ureeka	eureka
ureen	urine
urj	urge
Urope	Europe
urrn	*earn, erne, urn*
useage	usage
useing	using
ushally	usually

WRONG	RIGHT
ushwal	usual
usirp	usurp
usirpashun	usurpation
Uta	Utah
utalize	utilize
uterance	utterance
uterrus	uterus
uthanasha	euthanasia
utilatarian	utilitarian
utilityes	utilities
utillize	utilize
Utopea	Utopia
utterence	utterance
uzury	usury

V

WRONG	RIGHT
vacanncy	vacancy
vacansees	vacancies
vacansy	vacancy
vaccum	vacuum
vaen	*vain, vane, vein*
vage	vague
vagrent	vagrant
vaiz	vase
vajina	vagina
vakansy	vacancy
vakashun	*vacation*
vaksinate	vaccinate
vaksination	vaccination
valadictorian	valedictorian
valease	valise

The asterisk (*) next to boldface words flags "misspellings" that are also real words. For words that appear in italics, see Part II, "Sound-Alikes and Confusibles," to confirm your word choice.

WRONG	RIGHT	WRONG	RIGHT
validaty	validity	Veena	Vienna
valoor	velour	veenal	*venal*
valosity	velocity	veenyal	*venial*
valt	*vault*	vegence	vengeance
valu	value	vegetible	vegetable
valubul	valuable	vehamense	vehemence
valyant	valiant	vehament	vehement
van Goe	Van Gogh	vehicul	vehicle
Vancoover	Vancouver	vehiculer	vehicular
vane*	*vain, vein*	vejatarian	vegetarian
vaneer	veneer	vejtable	vegetable
Vaneeshan	Venetian	velor	velour
vanella	vanilla	velosity	velocity
vankwish	vanquish	velvateen	velveteen
vaper	vapor	velvaty	velvety
varable	variable	venason	venison
varcity	varsity	venchur	venture
vareity	variety	venerble	venerable
vareous	various	Veneshan	Venetian
varience	*variance*	Venis	Venice
varietee	variety	venjence	vengeance
varry	*vary, very*	Venswaila	Venezuela
varyanse	*variance, variants*	ventalate	ventilate
varyus	various	ventracul	ventricle
vasal	*vassal*	ventrilaquist	ventriloquist
vasaleen	vaseline	venyou	venue
vasillate	vacillate	Veracruise	Veracruz
Vatacan	Vatican	verafacation	verification
vaudville	vaudeville	verafy	verify
vawnt	*vaunt*	verashus	*veracious*
vayl	*vale, veil*	verasity	*veracity*
vayn	*vain, vane, vein*	veratable	veritable
veamence	vehemence	verbage	verbiage
vech	vetch	verball	verbal

WRONG	RIGHT	WRONG	RIGHT
verbatum	verbatim	vijilance	vigilance
verchuosity	virtuosity	vijilant	vigilant
verile	*viral, virile*	vikar	vicar
verjin	virgin	viktum	victim
vermillion	vermilion	vil	*vial, vile, viol*
vermooth	vermouth	vilate	violate
vernakular	vernacular	vilence	violence
verry	*vary, very*	vilet	violet
vershun	version	vilij	village
versitile	versatile	villin	villain
vertabra	*vertebra, vertebrae*	vinager	vinegar
vertacal	vertical	vindacate	vindicate
vesel	*vessel*	vinel	vinyl
vespir	vesper	vinsable	vincible
vestabul	vestibule	violater	violator
vestij	vestige	violen	violin
vetenarian	veterinarian	viralence	virulence
veterin	veteran	viralent	virulent
veyl	*vale, veil*	viranda	veranda
viaduck	viaduct	virchew	*virtu, virtue*
vibrashun	vibration	virchewoso	virtuoso
vicarij	vicarage	virchewus	virtuous
vice*	vise	virchual	virtual
vicktoryus	victorious	virel	*viral, virile*
victer	victor	virj	verge
vidocassete	videocassette	virjin	virgin
viekareous	vicarious	virjinal	virginal
viel	*vial, vile, viol*	Virjinya	Virginia
vielate	violate	Virmont	Vermont
vieral	*viral, virile*	virnacular	vernacular
vigalantee	vigilante	visable	visible
vigerous	vigorous	visaj	visage
vijil	vigil	visatude	vicissitude

The asterisk (*) next to boldface words flags "misspellings" that are also real words. For words that appear in italics, see Part II, "Sound-Alikes and Confusibles," to confirm your word choice.

WRONG	RIGHT
visaversa	vice versa
viscis	*viscous*
vishun	vision
vishus	*vicious*
vishyal	visual
visinity	vicinity
visle	*vial, vile, viol*
vitalaty	vitality
vitemin	vitamin
vitreolic	vitriolic
vitul	vital
vivashus	vivacious
vizability	visibility
vizable	visible
vizator	visitor
vizer	visor
vizit	visit
vizual	visual
vocashun	*vocation*
vog	vogue
vois	voice
vokabulary	vocabulary
vokal	vocal
volatil	volatile
volee	volley
volishun	volition
volkano	volcano
voltij	voltage
volum	volume
vorashus	*voracious*
vorasity	*voracity*
vortecks	*vortex*
vosiferus	vociferous
voteing	voting

WRONG	RIGHT
vowl	vowel
voyjer	*voyager*
voyse	voice
voyur	*voyeur*
vulcanic	volcanic
vulcano	volcano
vulchur	vulture
vulger	vulgar
vulnerbul	vulnerable
vurchus	virtuous
vurj	verge
vyable	viable
vyce	*vice, vise*
vye	vie
vyolator	violator
vyse	*vice, vise*

W

WRONG	RIGHT
wach	watch
wack	whack
wade*	*weighed*
wafe	waif
waid	*wade, weighed*
waij	wage
waik	wake
wail*	*wale, whale*
wair	*ware, wear, where*
waist*	*waste*
wait*	*weight*
wajer	wager
waks	*wax, whacks*
walc	*walk*

WRONG	RIGHT
wale*	*wail, whale*
walet	wallet
walup	wallop
walz	waltz
want*	*wont*
war*	*wore*
warantee	*warrantee, warranty*
warbul	warble
ward*	*warred*
ware*	*wear, where*
warent	warrant
warever	wherever
warf	wharf
warn*	*worn*
warrantyes	warranties
warsh	wash
warshable	washable
wary*	*weary*
waryur	warrior
waste*	*waist*
wat	*watt, what*
wate	*wait, weight*
watermellon	watermelon
wauk	*walk, wok*
wave*	*waive*
waver*	*waiver*
wax*	*whacks*
waxey	waxy
way*	*weigh, whey*
wayd	*wade, weighed*
wayst	*waist, waste*
waytress	waitress
wayv	*waive, wave*

WRONG	RIGHT
wayver	*waiver, waver*
waz	was
wazn't	wasn't
we*	*wee*
weal*	*we'll, wheal, wheel*
wear*	*ware, where*
wearesome	wearisome
weed*	*we'd*
weedling	wheedling
week*	*weak*
weel	*weal, we'll, wheal, wheel*
weeld	wield
weener	wiener
weerd	weird
weery	*weary*
weet	wheat
weeve	*weave, we've*
weeze	wheeze
weezle	weasel
Wegwood	Wedgwood
weild	wield
weiv	*weave, we've*
wej	wedge
wel	*weal, we'll, wheal, wheel*
welp	whelp
welth	wealth
wen*	*when*
Wenzday	Wednesday
wepon	weapon
wer	*we're, weir*
wership	worship
werwolf	werewolf
West Verjinya	West Virginia

The asterisk (*) next to boldface words flags "misspellings" that are also real words. For words that appear in italics, see Part II, "Sound-Alikes and Confusibles," to confirm your word choice.

WRONG	RIGHT	WRONG	RIGHT
westurn .... western		**wim** .... whim
wet* .... *whet*		**wimen** .... women
wetest .... wettest		**wimper** .... whimper
wether* .... *weather, whether*		**wimsacal** .... whimsical
wey .... *way, weigh, whey*		**Winapeg** .... Winnipeg
wharever .... wherever		**winch*** .... *wench*
whayl .... *wail, wale, whale*		**windoe** .... widow
whearl .... *whirl*		**windyness** .... windiness
whedle .... wheedle		**wine*** .... *whine*
wheel* .... *weal, we'll, wheal*		**winned** .... *wind, wined*
wheezey .... wheezy		**winny** .... *whinny, whiny*
wheras .... whereas		**winow** .... winnow
whiney .... *whiny*		**winse** .... *wince, wins, winze*
whir .... *whirl*		**winsum** .... winsome
whitch .... *which, witch*		**wip** .... whip
whohp .... *whoop*		**wirl** .... *whirl, whorl*
whol .... *hole, whole*		**wirlygigs** .... whirligigs
wholy .... *holey, holy, wholly*		**wirm** .... worm
whoozy .... woozy		**wirry** .... worry
whor .... *hoar, hoer, whore*		**wirst** .... *worst, wurst*
whord .... *hoard, horde, whored*		**wisk** .... whisk
whos/whoz .... *who's, whose*		**wisker** .... whisker
whurl .... *whirl, whorl*		**wiskey** .... whiskey
Whyoming .... Wyoming		**Wiskonsin** .... Wisconsin
wich .... *which, witch*		**wisle** .... whistle
wiend .... *wind, wined*		**wisp** .... whisp
wierd .... weird		**wisper** .... whisper
wiet .... *white, wight*		**wispered** .... whispered
wiff .... whiff		**wist** .... whist
wiked .... wicked		**wisteeria** .... wisteria
wikit .... wicket		**wistle** .... whistle
wile* .... *while*		**wit*** .... *whit*
wilful .... willful		**witch*** .... *which*
willoe .... willow		**wite** .... *white, wight*

WRONG	RIGHT	WRONG	RIGHT
witheld	withheld	**worp**	warp
wither	whither	**worresome**	worrisome
witherz	withers	**Worshington**	Washington
withold	withhold	**wrak**	*rack, wrack*
witish	whitish	**wraped**	*rapped, rapt, wrapped*
wittasism	witticism	**wraut**	wrought
wittle	whittle	**wrech**	*retch, wretch*
wiz	whiz	**wrek**	*reck, wreck*
wize	wise	**wri**	*rye, wry*
wizerd	wizard	**wrigler**	wriggler
woful	woeful	**wrinch**	*wrench*
wok*	*walk*	**write***	*right, wright*
won*	*one*	**writen**	written
wonse	*once*	**writting**	writing
wont*	*won't*	**writz**	*ritz, writs*
wonton	won ton	**wroat**	*rote, wrote*
wood*	*would*	**wuf/wulf**	wolf
woolfsbain	wolfsbane	**wuman**	woman
woollen	woolen	**wunder**	wonder
woolvereen	wolverine	**wunderful**	wonderful
wooly	woolly	**wundrus**	wondrous
woom	womb	**wuns**	*once*
woond	wound	**wurld**	world
wooped	whooped	**wurn't**	weren't
Woostersher	Worcestershire	**wurse**	worse
wopper	whopper	**wurst***	*worst*
wor	*war*	**wut**	*watt, what*
wordaj	wordage	**wy**	why
worden	warden	**wyle**	*while, wile*
worf	wharf	**wynch**	*winch*
workdai	*workday*	**wyr**	*weir, we're*
workeday	*workaday*	**wythdraw**	withdraw
worn*	*warn*		

The asterisk (*) next to boldface words flags "misspellings" that are also real words. For words that appear in italics, see Part II, "Sound-Alikes and Confusibles," to confirm your word choice.

WRONG	RIGHT

X

WRONG	RIGHT
xacushun	execution
xacute	execute
xacutioner	executioner
xalt	*exalt*
xaust	exhaust
xcept	*except*
xcess	*excess*
xchange	exchange
xclaim	exclaim
xclamation	exclamation
xclude	exclude
xclushun	exclusion
xclusive	exclusive
xclusively	exclusively
xcrament	excrement
xcree	excrete
xcrusheating	excruciating
xcurshun	excursion
xcusability	excusability
xcusable	excusable
xcuse	excuse
xecutive	execute
xecutricks	executrix
xekutive	executive
xekutor	executor
xemplary	exemplary
xersise	*exercise*
xhabishun	exhibition
xibit	exhibit
xilerate	exhilarate

WRONG	RIGHT
xilerates	exhilarates
xit	exit
xofisheo	ex officio
xonerate	exonerate
xorbatent	exorbitant
xorcise	*exorcise*
xorted	exhorted
xotic	exotic
xpand	*expand*
xpatriot	expatriate
xpedient	expedient
xpedishun	expedition
xpedite	expedite
xpel	expel
xpend	*expend*
xpendichur	expenditure
xpense	expense
xperament	experiment
xperience	experience
xpert	expert
xpesive	expensive
xpiration	expiration
xpire	expire
xplain	explain
xplanation	explanation
xpletive	expletive
xplisit	*explicit*
xplode	explode
xploit	exploit
xploration	exploration
xplore	explore
xportation	exportation
xpose	expose
xpound	*expound*

WRONG	RIGHT	WRONG	RIGHT
xpoza	expose	**xtreem**	extreme
xpress	express	**xtricate**	extricate
xpropriate	expropriate	**xtrordinary**	extraordinary
xpulshun	expulsion	**xtrude**	extrude
xpunj	expunge	**xuberence**	exuberance
xsellence	excellence	**xuberent**	exuberant
xsellent	excellent	**xult**	*exult*
xsels	excels	**xylaphone**	xylophone
xsepshun	exception		
xseptionable	*exceptionable*		
xseptional	*exceptional*		

Y

WRONG	RIGHT	WRONG	RIGHT
xserpt	excerpt		
xsess	*excess*	**yamalka**	yarmulke
xsise	excise	**yamer**	yammer
xsishun	excision	**yaro**	yarrow
xsite	excite	**yaun**	yawn
xsitement	excitement	**yaut**	yacht
xtant	*extant, extent*	**yeeld**	yield
xteerior	exterior	**yeelding**	yielding
xtemparaneous		**yeer**	year
	extemporaneous	**yeild**	yield
xtension	extension	**yello**	yellow
xtent	*extant, extent*	**yern**	yearn
xtenuate	extenuate	**yernings**	yearnings
xterminate	exterminate	**yestirday**	yesterday
xtersensory	extrasensory	**yewser friendly**	user-friendly
xtingwish	extinguish	**yodul**	yodel
xtink	extinct	**yoge**	yogi
xtirpate	extirpate	**yogert**	yogurt
xtract	extract	**yoke***	*yolk*
xtradite	extradite	**Yom Kiper**	Yom Kippur
xtraneous	extraneous	**yoo**	*ewe, yew, you*
xtravagance	extravagance	**yoonacorn**	unicorn

The asterisk (*) next to boldface words flags "misspellings" that are also real words. For words that appear in italics, see Part II, "Sound-Alikes and Confusibles," to confirm your word choice.

WRONG	RIGHT	WRONG	RIGHT
yoonaform	uniform	zar	czar or tsar
yoonason	unison	Zavier	Xavier
yoonaversal	universal	zeel	zeal
yoonaversity	university	zeenith	zenith
yoonit	unit	zeero	zero
yoonity	unity	zefer	zephyr
yoosij	usage	zelot	zealot
yooth	youth	zelus	*zealous*
yore*	*your, you're*	zeneth	zenith
Yosamite	Yosemite	zenofobia	xenophobia
you*	*ewe, yew*	zenya	zinnia
youker	euchre	zepalin	zeppelin
Youkon	Yukon	zerography	xerography
youl	*you'll, yule*	Zerox	Xerox
Youma	Yuma	zigote	zygote
your*	*yore, you're*	zilophone	xylophone
yous	use	zink	zinc
yousable	usable or useable	ziper	zipper
yowel	yowl	zirconeum	zirconium
Yugaslavia	Yugoslavia	zoan	zone
yuka	yucca	zodeack	zodiac
Yukatan	Yucatan	zoeology	zoology
yul	*you'll, yule*	zomby	zombie
yumy	yummy	zoneing	zoning
yunanimity	unanimity	zooalonjacal	zoological
Yung	Jung	zookene	zucchini
yungster	youngster	zue	zoo
yurin	urine	zume	zoom
yuth	youth	Zurick	Zurich

Z

Zuss	Zeus
zwiback	zwieback
zylophone	xylophone

zanney .... zany

Part II

Sound-Alikes and Confusibles

A

a lot many; parcel of land; to decide by chance
allot to distribute by lot or in arbitrary shares

a while *n.* a time (for *a while*)
awhile *adv.* for a short time

abduct to kidnap
adduct to pull toward axis

abjure to renounce
adjure to command

absorb to suck up
adsorb to collect in condensed form

absorption act of being sucked up
adsorption act of adhesion to a surface

accede to agree
exceed to go beyond limits

accept to take
except to exclude

access ability to enter
assess to evaluate excess surplus
excess surplus

acme highest point
acne skin disorder

acts deeds
ax cutting tool
axe cutting tool

ad advertisement
add to increase

adapt to make fit
adept skilled; proficient
adopt to take as one's own

add, ad
See *ad, add*

addition something added
edition form in which something is published

adduct, abduct
See *abduct, adduct*

adept, adopt, adapt
See *adapt, adept, adopt*

adherence act of sticking; devotion
adherents followers

adieu farewell
ado fuss about

adjoin to be next to
adjourn to postpone; recess

adjure, abjure
See *abjure, adjure*

ado, adieu
See *adieu, ado*

adolescence state or process of
    growing up
adolescents young people;
    teenagers

adopt, adapt, edept
See *adapt, adept, adopt*

adsorb, absorb
See *absorb, adsorb*

adsorption, absorption
See *absorption, adsorption*

adverse unfavorable
averse disinclined

advice recommendation
advise to recommend

aerie bird nest on a cliff
airy of or relating to air; light

affect *n.* emotion or feeling; *v.* to
    influence
effect *n.* result; *v.* to accomplish

affluent rich; abundant
effluent outflowing

aid help
aide assistant

ail to be unwell
ale malt beverage

air atmosphere
ere before (poetic)
heir one who inherits

airy, aerie
See *aerie, airy*

aisle passageway or corridor
I'll contraction of *I will*
isle island

ale, ail
See *ail, ale*

align to bring into line
A-line having a flared bottom

alimentary of or relating to
    nourishment
elementary basic; fundamental

A-line, align
See *align, A-line*

all whole number or amount
awl pointed tool

all ready completely ready
already so soon

all together together; in concert
altogether wholly; thoroughly

all ways total number of methods
always at all times; invariably

allay to alleviate
alley narrow back street
alloy *n.* mixture of metals; *v.* to debase by mixing
ally *n.* associate; *v.* to enter into an alliance

alleys narrow back streets
allies partners; associates

allot, a lot
See *a lot, allot*

allowed permitted
aloud spoken

allusion reference
elision omitting something
illusion misleading image

ally, allay, alley, alloy
See *allay, alley, alloy, ally*

aloud, allowed
See *allowed, aloud*

already, all ready
See *all ready, already*

altar platform in a church
alter to change

alternate *n.* substitute; *v.* to do or use by turns
alternative additional choice; option

altitude height
attitude posture; mental position

altogether, all together
See *all together, altogether*

always, all ways
See *all ways, always*

amend to modify
emend to edit or correct

analyst one who analyzes
annalist writer of annals; historian

androgen type of steroid that acts as a male hormone
androgyne androgynous plant

anecdote short narrative
antedate to precede in time
antidote agent to counteract poison

anergy condition in which body fails to respond to antigen
energy capacity for vigorous action

angel heavenly spirit; good or lovely person
angle *n* space between two lines that meet; *v* to fish with hook and line

annalist, analyst
See *analyst, annalist*

annual once a year; publication appearing yearly; plant that lives one year
annul to make void; to destroy the force of

ant insect
aunt sister of one's mother or
  father

ante- before
anti- against

antedate, anecdote, antidote
See *anecdote, antedate, antidote*

anti-, ante-
See *ante-, anti-*

antidote, antedate, anecdote
See *anecdote, antedate, antidote*

any one any individual person or
  thing with stress on *one*
anyone any person with stress on
  any

any way any method or process
anyway anyhow; nevertheless

apposite highly pertinent
opposite occupying opposing
  positions

appraise to estimate the value of
apprise to notify
apprize to value; to appreciate

approximate nearly correct or
  exact
proximate very close; forthcoming

arc something arched or curved
ark boat; something affording
  protection

arraign to bring before a court to
  answer an indictment
arrange to put in proper order

arraignment charge
arrangement something arranged

arrange, arraign
See *arraign, arrange*

arrangement, arraignment
See *arraignment, arrangement*

arrant extreme
errant traveling; straying

arteriosclerosis abnormal
  thickening and loss of elasticity
  of arteries
atherosclerosis form of arteriosclerosis that includes fat
  deposits

ascent act of rising or mounting
  upwards
assent acquiescence

assay to evaluate
essay composition

assent, ascent
See *ascent, assent*

assess, excess, access
See *access, assess, excess*

assistance help
assistants helpers

assure to make certain (followed by a person)
ensure to make certain; to insure (followed by *that*)
insure to give, take, or procure insurance on; to protect

ate past tense of *eat*
eight number

atherosclerosis, arteriosclerosis
See *arteriosclerosis, atherosclerosis*

attendance act or fact of attending
attendants attendees

attitude, altitude
See *altitude, attitude*

auger tool
augur to predict

aught zero; cipher
ought indicating obligation or duty

augur, auger
See *auger, augur*

aunt, ant
See *ant, aunt*

aural relating to the ear or hearing
oral spoken

auricle chamber of the heart
oracle wise person who states prophecies

averse, adverse
See *adverse, averse*

avert to turn away; to prevent
evert to turn outward or inside out

avocation hobby
vacation period for rest and relaxation
vocation work in which one is regularly employed

away from this or that place
aweigh raised clear of (anchor)

awful inspiring awe; terrible
offal entrails of slaughtered animals; refuse or garbage

awhile, a while
See *a while, awhile*

awl, all
See *all, awl*

ax, acts, axe
See *acts, ax, axe*

aye yes
eye organ of sight
I personal pronoun

B

bad below standard; evil
bade past tense of *bid*

bail *n.* security for appearance of prisoner; *v.* to clear water out of a boat
bale *n.* large bundle of goods; *v.* to make into bundles

baited nagged; set a trap
bated restrained; reduced

bald lacking natural covering
baud computer transmission speed
    in terms of bits per second
bawled cried loudly; bellowed

bale, bail
See *bail, bale*

ball a round object used in games;
    formal party with dancing
bawl *n.* a shout; *v.* to cry loudly

band something that constricts or
    binds; musicians
banned prohibited

banns public announcement (of
    marriage)
bans *n.* prohibitions *v.* prohibits

bard poet
barred having bars; excluded

bare to uncover or reveal
bear *n.* animal; *v.* to carry

baring uncovering
barring fastening with a bar;
    excepting
bearing carrying; enduring

baron nobleman
barren incapable of producing
    offspring

barred, bard
See *bard, barred*

barren, baron
See *baron, barren*

barring, baring, bearing
See *baring, barring, bearing*

basal of, at, or forming a base
basil garden herb

base foundation
bass deep tone; fish

based made or formed to serve as a
    base
baste to sew with loose stitches; to
    moisten at intervals

bases plural of *base* or *basis*
basis foundation

basil, basal
See *basal, basil*

basis, bases
See *bases, basis*

bass, base
See *base, bass*

baste, based
See *based, baste*

bated, baited
See *baited, bated*

baud, bald, bawled
See *bald, baud, bawled*

bawl, ball
See *ball, bawl*

bawled, bald, baud
See *bald, baud, bawled*

bazaar marketplace
bizarre strange

be to exist
bee insect; meeting to work or
    compete

bear, bare
See *bare, bear*

bearing, baring, barring
See *baring, barring, bearing*

beat to strike repeatedly
beet vegetable

bee, be
See *be, bee*

been form of verb *to be*
bin box for storage

beer malt beverage
bier coffin or its stand

beet, beat
See *beat, beet*

bel ten decibels
bell a hollow device that gives a
    tone when struck
belle popular, attractive woman

berry small fruit
bury to inter or conceal

berth place to sleep; allotted space
birth emergence; beginning

beside alongside of; next to
besides in addition to

better of higher quality
bettor one who bets

biannual occurring twice a year
biennial occurring every two years

bier, beer
See *beer, bier*

bight corner, bend, or angle
bite *n.* morsel; wound made with
    the mouth; *v.* to seize with teeth
byte sequence of adjacent binary
    digits

billed past tense of *bill*
build to construct

bin, been
See *been, bin*

bird feathered, egg-laying
    vertebrate
burred having burs

birth, berth
See *berth, birth*

bite, bight, byte
See *bight, bite, byte*

bizarre, bazaar
See *bazaar, bizarre*

blew past tense of *blow*
blue color

bloc grouping
block obstruction

blond flaxen color; light-haired man
blonde flaxen color; light-haired woman

blue, blew
See *blew, blue*

boar male hog
boor rude or insensitive person
bore one who causes boredom

board plank; daily meals; directors
bored pierced with a rotary tool; weary with tedium

boarder one who is provided with regular meals
border boundary or frontier; edge

bode to foretell or presage
bowed shaped like a bow

bolder more bold
boulder large stone

bole tree trunk
boll pod or capsule of a plant
bowl vessel for holding liquids; game

boor, boar, bore
See *boar, boor, bore*

border, boarder
See *boarder, border*

bore, boar, boor
See *boar, boor, bore*

bored, board
See *board, bored*

born came alive
borne carried
bourn stream or brook

borough division of an urban area
burro donkey
burrow hole made by an animal

bough tree branch
bow to bend or yield

bouillon broth
bullion gold or silver in bulk

boulder, bolder
See *bolder, boulder*

bourn, born, borne
See *born, borne, bourne*

bow, bough
See *bough, bow*

bowed, bode
See *bode, bowed*

bowl, bole, boll
See *bole, boll, bowl*

boy male child
buoy float

braid cord having three or more component strands
brayed uttered cry of a donkey

braise to cook slowly with little moisture
braze to solder

brake to slow and stop
break to fracture

brayed, braid
See *braid, brayed*

braze, braise
See *braise, braze*

breach break
breech buttocks

bread food baked from dough
bred past tense of *breed*

breadth expanse
breath air inhaled
breathe to inhale

break, brake
See *brake, break*

breath, breadth, breathe
See *breadth, breath, breathe*

bred, bread
See *bread, bred*

breech, breach
See *breach, breech*

brewed steeped; boiled; fermented
brood *n.* young of an animal; *v.* to incubate; to worry

brews *n.* brewed beverages; *v.* cooks
bruise contusion; abrasion

briar tobacco pipe made from brier root
brier thorny plant

bridal pertaining to a bride
bridle headgear for a horse

brier, briar
See *briar, brier*

broach to open or introduce
brooch pin or clasp

brood, brewed
See *brewed, brood*

bruise, brews
See *brews, bruise*

bruit clamor
brut very dry
brute beast; savage person

buccal pertaining to the cheek
buckle fastener

build, billed
See *billed, build*

bullion, bouillon
See *bouillon, bullion*

bundt type of tube pan with fluted sides
bunt *n.* disease of wheat; *v.* to bat lightly

buoy, boy
See *boy, buoy*

burred, bird
See *bird, burred*

burro, borough, burrow
See *borough, burro, burrow*

bury, berry
See *berry, bury*

bus large motor-driven vehicle
buss kiss

but except for; small amount; cutting edge of a tool; conjunction
butt *n.* thicker end of something; *v.* to thrust or push ahead

buy to purchase
by near
bye a side issue; term used in bridge; shortened *good-bye*

byte, bite, bight
See *bight, bite, byte*

C

cache hiding place; something hidden
cash ready money

calendar chart for reckoning time
calender machine for processing
colander device for draining food

callous hardened; unfeeling
callus thickened place on the skin

Calvary site of Jesus' crucifixion
cavalry mounted soldiers

can't contraction of *cannot*
cant jargon; trite or pious phrases

canapé appetizer
canopy awning

cannon gun
canon law

canopy, canapé
See *canapé, canopy*

cant, can't
See *can't, cant*

canvas cloth
canvass to solicit opinions

capital economic resources; seat of government
capitol legislature building

carat unit of weight
caret wedge-shaped mark
carrot vegetable

carousel something that revolves like a merry-go-round
carrousel game with thrown lances and chalk balls

carrot, carat, caret
See *carat, caret, carrot*

carrousel, carousel
See *carousel, carrousel*

cash, cache
See *cache, cash*

cast mold; a rigid dressing; actors
caste division of society

casual informal
causal expressing or indicating cause

cavalry, Calvary
See *Calvary, cavalry*

cease to stop
seas bodies of water
sees *n.* church positions of authority; *v.* to perceive with the eye
seize to grab

cede to yield or grant
seed *n.* part of a plant that will grow a new plant; *v.* to sow

ceiling overhead inside lining of a room
sealing closing or fastening

cell small compartment or unit
sell to give up in return for something else

cellar basement
seller one who sells

censer container for incense
censor one who cuts out objectionable material
censure to find fault with
sensor detection device

census numbering
senses faculties

cents monetary units; pennies
scents odors
sense meaning conveyed or intended

cereal grain; food product from grain
serial work appearing in parts at intervals

cession yielding; concession
session meeting or series of meetings

chafe to rub
chaff worthless matter

chased pursued
chaste pure

cheap inexpensive; stingy
cheep to chirp

chews masticates
choose to select

chic stylish
sheik Arab chief

choir group of singers
quire twenty-four sheets of paper

choose, chews
See *chews, choose*

choral relating to a chorus or choir
coral mass of marine animal skeletons
corral pen or enclosure for animals

chord harmonious tones blended together
cord rope, string, etc.; measure of wood

chute inclined plane or channel; slide
shoot new growth; firing of weapon

cirrous resembling cirrus clouds
cirrus wispy white cloud
serious sober; important; grave
serous of, relating to, or resembling serum

cite to quote
sight power of seeing
site place

clack chatter; clapping noise
claque group hired to applaud

Claus Santa
clause group of words
claws curved nails of an animal

click slight sharp noise
clique exclusive group of persons

climactic referring to a climax
climatic referring to a climate

climb to go upward
clime climate

clique, click
See *click, clique*

close *n.* conclusion; *v.* to shut
clothes covering for the body
cloths materials, usually woven

co-op cooperative
coop pen
coupe type of vehicle

coal kind of fuel
cole cabbage
kohl cosmetic to darken eyelids

coarse unrefined
course way or passage

cognation relationship by descent
cognition process of knowing

coin round piece of metal with a fixed value used as money
quoin external corner of a building

colander, calendar, calender
See *calendar, calender, colander*

cole, coal, kohl
See *coal, cole, kohl*

collage assembly of diverse fragments
college school

collision clash; impact
collusion secret agreement or cooperation

colonel commissioned officer
kernel central or essential part

coma state of profound unconsciousness
comma punctuation mark

comical funny
conical cone-shaped

comma, coma
See *coma, comma*

command to dominate; to order
commend to praise; to recommend

commence to begin or start
comments remarks

complacence calm and secure satisfaction
complaisance disposition to please or comply

complement something that completes
compliment expression of esteem; flattering remark

comprehensible understandable
comprehensive extensive; complete

confidant male to whom secrets are entrusted
confidante female to whom secrets are entrusted
confident full of conviction or assurance

confidentially in private
confidently with confidence; positively

confirmation act or process of confirming
conformation producing conformity; adaptation

conical, comical
See *comical, conical*

conscience consciousness of right or wrong
conscious perceiving or noticing; awake

consul diplomat
council assembly
counsel *n.* advice; lawyer; *v.* to advise

contagious carrying or liable to transmit
contiguous in physical contact

continual steady, with occasional breaks
continuous uninterrupted

coo soft cry
coup a brilliant, sudden, and usually successful stroke

coop, coupe, co-op
See *co-op, coop, coupe*

cops *n.* slang for police; *v.* seizes, wins, or steals
copse thicket of small trees or shrubs

copyrighter one who holds exclusive rights to a book, play, etc.
copywriter writer of ads and promotional material

cor exclamation of surprise
core center
corps group of persons
corpse dead body

coral, choral, corral
See *choral, coral, corral*

cord, chord
See *chord, cord*

core, corps, corpse, cor
See *cor, core, corps, corpse*

corespondents persons charged with adultery with defendant in divorce suit
correspondence communication by letters
correspondents those with whom one communicates

corporal *n.* officer; *adj* of or affecting the body
corporeal physical; not spiritual or intangible

corps, corpse, core, cor
See *cor, core, corps, corpse*

corral, coral, choral
See *choral, coral, corral*

correspondence, correspondents, corespondents
See *corespondents, correspondence, correspondents*

costume clothing
custom usual practice

council, consul, counsel
See *consul, council, counsel*

councillor member of a council
counselor advisor; lawyer

counsel, consul, council
See *consul, council, counsel*

counselor , councillor
See *councillor, counselor*

coup, coo
See *coo, coup*

coupe, coop, co-op
See *co-op, coop, coupe*

course, coarse
See *coarse, course*

cousin son or daughter of one's aunt or uncle
cozen to cheat or defraud

coward one who lacks courage
cowered shrank or crouched quivering with fear

cozen, cousin
See *cousin, cozen*

craft skill or trade; boat
kraft strong paper or board made from wood pulp

creak grating or rasping noise
creek small stream
crick painful spasmodic condition of muscles in the back or neck

cream yellowish high-butterfat part of milk
crème cream; liqueur

credible plausible
creditable worthy of belief, esteem, or praise

creek, creak, crick
See *creak, creek, crick*

crème, cream
See *cream, crème*

crevasse deep crack or fissure
crevice narrow opening caused by a crack or split

crewel yarn used for embroidery
cruel inhumane; mean

crews company of people associated together
cruise tour, usually by ship

crick, creak, creek
See *creak, creek, crick*

critic one who expresses judgment
critique act of criticizing; review

cruel, crewel
See *crewel, cruel*

cruise, crews
See *crews, cruise*

cubical cube-shaped
cubicle small compartment

cue hint; rod used in billiards
queue line

currant small seedless raisin
current flow, usually marked by force or strength

curser one who curses
cursor blinking indicator that marks one's current position on a computer screen

custom, costume
See *costume, custom*

cymbal plate that produces a clashing musical tone
symbol token of identity; visible sign

D

dairy milk farm
diary daily record book

dam to check the flow, especially of water
damn to condemn strongly; to curse

days plural of *day*
daze *n.* bewilderment; *v.* to stun

dear beloved; expensive
deer animal

debauch to seduce; to debase
debouch to march out into open ground

deceased dead
diseased unhealthy

decent respectable; fit; modest
descent act of descending
dissent disagreement

decree law
degree step; grade

deer, dear
See *dear, deer*

defalcation act of embezzlement
defecation discharge from the bowels
defection abandonment of allegiance or duty

deference respect; esteem; yielding
difference quality or state of being unlike
diffidence shyness; hesitancy through lack of self-confidence

deferential showing deference or respect
differential difference between comparable individuals or classes

degree, decree
See *decree, degree*

demur to object
demure reserved; modest
demurrer pleading at law

dense thick; stupid
dents depressions or nicks

dependence state of being influenced or supported by another
dependents persons relying on another for support

deposition written statement
disposition temperament; outcome

depravation depravity
deprivation loss

deprecate to express disapproval of
depreciate to lower in value

deprivation, depravation
See *depravation, deprivation*

descent, decent, dissent
See *decent, descent, dissent*

desert *n.* arid region; *v.* to abandon
dessert final course of a meal

deserts deserved reward or punishment
desserts plural of *dessert*

desolate sad
dissolute having loose morals

desperate having lost hope
disparate markedly different

dessert, desert
See *desert, dessert*

desserts, deserts
See *deserts, desserts*

detract to take away from or lower the value of
distract to divert attention

device scheme; contrivance
devise to form in mind; to invent; to bequeath

devisor one who bequeaths property in a will
divisor number by which a dividend is divided

dew moisture, especially in droplets
do to act
due owing

dialectal of a dialect
dialectic of logical argumentation

diary, dairy
See *dairy, diary*

die to cease to live
dye to color

difference, diffidence, deference
See *deference, difference, diffidence*

differential, deferential
See *deferential, differential*

diffidence, deference, difference
See *deference, diffidence, difference*

diner one who dines; dining car; small restaurant
dinner a meal

dinghy small boat
dingy dirty; discolored

dinner, diner
See *diner, dinner*

diplomat one employed or skilled in diplomacy
diplomate one who holds a diploma, especially a physician

disapprove to express an unfavorable opinion of; to reject
disprove to prove false

disassemble to take apart
dissemble to assume a false appearance

disburse to pay out
disperse to break up; to spread

disc phonograph record; working part of plow; various rounded anatomical structures
disk coated plate for storing computer data; thin circular object

discomfit to confuse or frustrate
discomfort to make uncomfortable

discreet circumspect; prudent
discrete separate

discus heavy, circular plate thrown as a test of skill
discuss to talk over

diseased, deceased
See *deceased, diseased*

disillusion to leave without illusion
dissolution disintegration

disinterested impartial
uninterested lacking interest; bored

disk, disc
See *disc, disk*

disparate, desperate
See *desperate, disparate*

disperse, disburse
See *disburse, disperse*

disposition, deposition
See *deposition, disposition*

disprove, disapprove
See *disapprove, disprove*

dissemble, disassemble
See *disassemble, dissemble*

dissent, decent, descent
See *decent, descent, dissent*

dissidence dissent; disagreement
dissidents those who differ or
    disagree

dissolute, desolate
See *desolate, dissolute*

dissolution, disillusion
See *disillusion, dissolution*

distract, detract
See *detract, distract*

divers *n.* plural of *diver;*
    adj. various
diverse differing from one another

divisor, deviser
See *deviser, divisor*

do, dew, due
See *dew, do, due*

doe female deer
dough flour mixture; money

done finished
dun *n.* demand for payment; *adj*
    drab color

dose measured amount
doze to sleep

dough, doe
See *doe, dough*

dual of two
duel fight

ducked lowered (as head); evaded
duct tube or pipe

due, dew, do
See *dew, do, due*

duel, dual
See *dual, duel*

dun, done
See *done, dun*

dunnage packing material around
    cargo
tonnage capacity in tons

dye, die
See *die, dye*

dyeing coloring
dying expiring

earn to receive in return for effort
erne white-tailed sea eagle
urn ornamental vase

earnest serious; grave
Ernest masculine name

edition, addition
See *addition, edition*

educable capable of being educated
educible able to elicit or bring out

eerie weird
Erie name of a lake or city

effect, affect
See *affect, effect*

effluent, affluent
See *affluent, effluent*

eight, ate
See *ate, eight*

either one or the other
ether gas

elementary, alimentary
See *alimentary, elementary*

elicit to draw forth or bring out
illicit unlawful

eligible qualified to be chosen
illegible indecipherable
legible capable of being read

elision, allusion, illusion
See *allusion, elision, illusion*

elusive evading grasp or pursuit
illusive illusory; deceptive

emend, amend
See *amend, emend*

emerge to come up; to come into view
immerge to plunge into; to immerse

emigrant one who leaves one's country
immigrant one who comes to a country to take up residence

emigrate to leave a country
immigrate to enter and settle in a country

eminent renowned
immanent inherent
imminent about to happen

emission act of emitting
omission something left out

empathize to share in another's thoughts, emotions, or feelings
emphasize to give emphasis to; to stress

endemic native; restricted to a locality
epidemic widespread contagion

endogenous developing from within
indigenous existing, growing, or produced naturally in a region or country

energy, anergy
See *anergy, energy*

enervate to lessen vitality or strength of
innervate to supply with nerves

ensure, insure, assure
See *assure, ensure, insure*

enter come in
inter bury

enthrall to hold spellbound
in thrall in bondage

entomology study of insects
etymology history of words

envelop to enclose or enfold
envelope flat (usually paper)
    container for a letter

epic long narrative poem
epoch point or period of time

epidemic, endemic
See *endemic, epidemic*

epigram witty saying
epigraph quotation suggesting a
    theme

epitaph inscription on a tomb
epithet descriptive term, often
    disparaging

epoch, epic
See *epic, epoch*

equable uniform
equitable fair; just

erasable capable of being erased
irascible hot-tempered

eraser rubber or felt used for
    removing marks
erasure act of removing or rubbing
    out

ere, air, heir
See *air, ere, heir*

Erie, eerie
See *eerie, Erie*

erne, earn, urn
See *earn, erne, urn*

Ernest, earnest
See *earnest, Ernest*

errant, arrant
See *arrant, errant*

erupt to burst forth
irrupt to rush in forcibly

essay, assay
See *assay, essay*

estop to bar; to prevent
stop to cease activity

ether, either
See *either, ether*

ethics moral principles or values
ethnics members of a minority
    group

etiology cause or origin
ideology a systematic body of
    concepts

etymology, entomology
See *entomology, etymology*

euphemism using less distasteful
    or offensive words
euphuism artificial, affected, high-
    flown style of speaking

evert, avert
See *avert, evert*

every day each day
everyday daily, with *every* stressed

every one every person, with the
  one stressed
everyone everybody, with *every*
  stressed

everyday, every day
See *every day, everyday*

everyone, every one
See *every one, everyone*

ewe female sheep
yew evergreen tree or shrub
you personal pronoun

exalt to raise high; to glorify
exult to rejoice

exceed, accede
See *accede, exceed*

except, accept
See *accept, except*

exceptionable objectionable
exceptional rare; better than
  average

excess, access, assess
See *access, assess, excess*

exercise to use; to exert oneself
  physically or mentally
exorcise to expel, as an evil spirit

expand to increase; to enlarge
expend to spend; to consume
expound to set forth or explain; to
  defend

explicit full, clear expression;
  without ambiguity
implicit implied

expound, expand, expend
See *expand, expend, expound*

extant in existence
extent range; limit

exult, exalt
See *exalt, exult*

eye, aye, I
See *aye, eye, I*

eyelet small hole
islet island

F

facet surface
faucet device with a valve for
  regulating the flow of liquid

factious promoting dissension
factitious artificial
fictitious imaginary; false

faille ribbed soft fabric
file device for keeping papers in
  order

fain happy; pleased
feign to pretend

faint to lose consciousness
feint to make a deceptive movement

fair *n.* festival; *adj* impartial; attractive
fare price charged to transport a person

fairy elf; imaginary being
ferry type of boat

faker one that fakes
fakir Hindu ascetic

fare, fair
See *fair, fare*

farther at or to a greater distance
further in addition; moreover

fate destiny
fete festival

faucet, facet
See *facet, faucet*

faun mythological half man, half goat
fawn young deer

fay fairy; elf
fey crazy; touched; able to see the future

faze to disconcert
phase stage or aspect

feat notable act or achievement
feet plural of *foot*

feign, fain
See *fain, feign*

feint, faint
See *faint, feint*

ferment to undergo certain chemical reactions
foment to incite

ferrule metal ring or cap
ferule rod for punishing children

ferry, fairy
See *fairy, ferry*

ferule, ferrule
See *ferrule, ferule*

fervor great warmth of emotion; zeal
furvor dandruff

fete, fate
See *fate, fete*

fey, fay
See *fay, fey*

fiance man engaged to be married
fiancee woman engaged to be married

fictitious, factious, factitious
See *factious, factitious, fictitious*

file, faille
See *faille, file*

filter device for removing suspended matter
philter love potion

finale end
finally at last; at the end
finely closely; in a fine way

find to come upon accidentally
fined subjected to a penalty

finely, finale, finally
See *finale, finally, finely*

firs evergreen trees
furs pelts; coats
furze European shrub

fiscal financial
physical having material existence

fisher one that fishes
fissure separation; crack

fizz hissing sound; carbonation
phiz face or facial expression

flack press agent
flak antiaircraft guns; dissention

flagrant glaring; conspicuously bad
fragrant having a pleasant odor

flair aptitude; style
flare to burn; to burst out

flak, flack
See *flack, flak*

flanges ribs or rims for strength
phalanges fingers or toes

flare, flair
See *flair, flare*

flaunt to make a boastful display
flout to treat with contempt

flea insect
flee to run away

flecks tiny spots or streaks
flex to bend

flee, flea
See *flea, flee*

flew past tense of *fly*
flu influenza; viral disease
flue enclosed passageway for
  directing a current

flex, flecks
See *flecks, flex*

floc mass resembling tufts of wool
flock group of birds or animals

flocks plural of *flock*
phlox creeping flower

floe large mass of floating ice
flow uninterrupted movement

flounder *n.* fish; *v.* to struggle
  awkwardly
founder to sink; to fail

flour finely ground grain
flower blossom

flout, flaunt
See *flaunt, flout*

flow, floe
See *floe, flow*

flower, flour
See *flour, flower*

flu, flew, flue
See *flew, flu, flue*

foaled gave birth to a colt
fold to lay one part over another

foggy filled with fog
fogy person with old-fashioned ideas

fold, foaled
See *foaled, fold*

foment, ferment
See *ferment, foment*

fondling caressing; petting
foundling abandoned child

for directed or sent to
fore front part of something
four number

forbear to abstain; to forgo
forebear ancestor

fore, four, for
See *for, fore, four*

forebear, forbear
See *forbear, forebear*

foreword an introductory statement to a book
forward at, toward, or of the front
froward not easily controlled; stubbornly willful

formally ceremoniously; conventionally
formerly previously

fort strong or fortified place
forte one's strong point

forth onward in time, place, or order
fourth number four in a series

forward, foreword, froward
See *foreword, forward, froward*

foul offensive
fowl bird, especially domestic

founder, flounder
See *flounder, founder*

foundling, fondling
See *fondling, foundling*

four, for, fore
See *for, fore, four*

fourth, forth
See *forth, fourth*

fowl, foul
See *foul, fowl*

fragrant, flagrant
See *flagrant, fragrant*

franc French monetary unit
frank forthright; honest

frantic emotionally out of control
frenetic frenzied

frays brawls; fights
phrase group of grammatically related words

frees turns loose; extricates
freeze to congeal into ice
frieze coarse woolen fabric; decoration or ornamental band on a building

frenetic, frantic
See *frantic, frenetic*

friar member of a religious order
fryer something used for frying;
  young chicken

frieze, frees, freeze
See *frees, freeze, frieze*

froward, forward, foreword
See *foreword, forward, froward*

fryer, friar
See *friar, fryer*

funeral burial ceremony
funereal relating to a funeral;
  solemn

furvur, fervor
See *fervor, furvor*

furry covered with fur
fury violent anger

furs, firs, furze
See *firs, furs, furze*

further, farther
See *farther, further*

fury, furry
See *furry, fury*

furze, firs, furs
See *firs, furs, furze*

G

gaff sharp hook for spearing fish
gaffe social blunder

gage token of defiance; glove
  thrown to the ground
gauge measure

gait manner of walking
gate opening in a wall or fence

galosh high overshoe
goulash kind of stew

gamble to bet
gambol to frolic

gantlet punishment; where two
  railroad tracks overlap
gauntlet glove covered with metal
  plates

gate, gait
See *gait, gate*

gauge, gage
See *gage, gauge*

gauntlet, gantlet
See *gantlet, gauntlet*

genes genetic units
jeans denim trousers

genius one with exceptional gifts
  or intelligence
genus kind, sort, or class

gentile non-Jewish (often specifically Christian)
gentle soft; not harsh

genus, genius
See *genius, genus*

gibe to reproach with taunting words
jibe to be in accord
jive to fool

gild to overlay with gold
guild association of craftsmen

gilt gold or something resembling it
guilt fact of having committed an offense

gist point of the matter
jest joke

glacier huge mass of ice
glazier one who glazes

gluey sticky; like glue
gooey messy; sticky

gorilla ape
guerrilla one who engages in irregular warfare

goulash, galosh
See *galosh, goulash*

gourd any of the ornamental, inedible fruits of a climbing plant
gourde basic monetary unity of Haiti

gourmand one excessively fond of eating and drinking
gourmet connoisseur of food and drink

grader one who grades; machine that levels the ground
grater shredder or grinder
greater larger or more distinguished

graft something grafted; illegal gain
graph diagram or chart
graphed plotted on a graph

granite hard rock
granted past tense of *grant*

graph, graft, graphed
See *graft, graph, graphed*

grate a frame of parallel bars or lattice; fireplace
great large; distinguished

grater, greater, grader
See *grader, grater, greater*

grays/greys turns gray
graze to feed on growing herbage; to abrade or scratch

grease rendered animal fat
Greece Mediterranean country

great, grate
See *grate, great*

greater, grater, grader
See *grader, grater, greater*

Greece, grease
See *grease, Greece*

grill *n.* an informal restaurant;
v. to question intensely; to broil
on a grill;
grille grating forming a barrier or
screen

grip strong or tenacious grasp;
suitcase
gripe complaint
grippe flu

grisly inspiring horror or fear
gristly consisting of or containing
gristle
grizzly somewhat gray; kind of
bear

groan moan
grown mature

guarantee assurance of fulfillment
of a condition
guaranty warranty; guarantee

guerrilla, gorilla
See *gorilla, guerrilla*

guessed estimated
guest one receiving hospitality

guide to lead or direct
guyed steadied or reinforced with a
guy (rope or chain)

guild, gild
See *gild, guild*

guilt, gilt
See *gilt, guilt*

guise form or style of dress;
semblance
guys fellows; ropes, chains, etc., to
brace or guide

guyed, guide
See *guide, guyed*

guys, guise
See *guise, guys*

H

hail salute; welcome; precipitation
in the form of chunks of ice
hale healthy

hair threadlike growth
hare rabbit

hale, hail
See *hail, hale*

hall large room for assembly
haul to pull with force
haw hawthorne berry; direction to
turn left; vocalized pause

halve to divide in half
have to be in possession of

hangar shed for airplanes
hanger frame for hanging clothes

hare, hair
See *hair, hare*

hart male deer
heart organ of the body; core

haul, hall, haw
See *hall, haul, haw*

have, halve
See *halve, have*

haw, hall, haul
See *hall, haul, haw*

hay dried grass
hey expression of surprise; salutation

heal to cure
heel part of the foot
he'll contraction of *he will*

healthful promoting good health
healthy in good health

hear to perceive with the ear
here in or at this place

heard past tense of *hear*
herd *n.* many of the same kind of animal; *v.* to drive animals

hearsay something heard from another
heresy opinion or doctrine contrary to accepted beliefs

heart, hart
See *hart, heart*

heel, heal, he'll
See *heal, heel, he'll*

heir, air, ere
See *air, ere, heir*

herd, heard
See *heard, herd*

here, hear
See *hear, here*

heresy, hearsay
See *hearsay, heresy*

heroin narcotic drug
heroine principal female character

hew to cut with an ax
hue color; shade

hey, hay
See *hay, hey*

hi hello
hie to hasten
high tall

hide to conceal
hied hastened

hie, hi, high
See *hi, hie, high*

hied, hide
See *hide, hied*

high, hi, hie
See *hi, hie, high*

higher loftier
hire to employ

him personal pronoun
hymn song of praise to God

hippie nonconformist, usually young
hippy having big hips

hire, higher
See *higher, hire*

ho expression of surprise
hoe implement for cultivating

hoar frost
hoer one who hoes
whore prostitute

hoard to gather and store away
horde multitude
whored acted as a whore

hoarse rough or harsh in sound
horse equine quadruped

hoe, ho
See *ho, hoe*

hoer, hoar, whore
See *hoar, hoer, whore*

hoes uses a hoe
hose stockings; flexible tube

hold to maintain possession
holed made a hole

hole hollowed-out place or cavity
whole entire; intact

holey containing holes
holy sacred
wholly completely; entirely

home *n.* house; *v.* to go home; to
    proceed toward objective
hone to sharpen

homely plain
homey homelike
homily sermon

hone, home
See *home, hone*

hoop ring; circular strip
whoop loud yell

horde, whored, hoard
See *hoard, horde, whored*

horse, hoarse
See *hoarse, horse*

hose, hoes
See *hoes, hose*

hostel place offering sleeping
    accommodations for travelers
hostile unfriendly; antagonistic

hours sixty-minute periods
ours yours and mine

hue, hew
See *hew, hue*

human of or relating to a person
humane marked by compassion

humerus long bone of the upper
    arm
humorous funny

hymn, him
See *him, hymn*

hyper- above or beyond
hypo- less than or below normal

I

I, aye, eye
See *aye, eye, I*

I'll, aisle, isle
See *aisle, I'll, isle*

ideal standard of perfection
idle inactive
idol image of a god
idyll narrative poem; romantic
interlude

ideology, etiology
See *etiology, ideology*

illegible, eligible, legible
See *eligible, illegible, legible*

illicit, elicit
See *elicit, illicit*

illusion, allusion, elision
See *allusion, elision, illusion*

illusive, elusive
See *elusive, illusive*

immanent, imminent, eminent
See *eminent, immanent, imminent*

immerge, emerge
See *emerge, immerge*

immigrant, emigrant
See *emigrant, immigrant*

immigrate, emigrate
See *emigrate, immigrate*

imminent, eminent, immanent
See *eminent, immanent, imminent*

immoral not moral
immortal exempt from death or
oblivion

immunity state of being protected
from a disease
impunity exemption or freedom
from punishment or harm

impassable incapable of being
passed or traveled
impassible incapable of feeling
pain
impossible incapable of occurring

implicit, explicit
See *explicit, implicit*

impossible, impassable, impassible
See *impassable, impassible, impossible*

impracticable impossible to put
into practice; very hard to
manage
impractical not useful; not showing good sense

impugn to assail or oppose
impute to attribute; to lay blame

impunity, immunity
See *immunity, impunity*

impute, impugn
See *impugn, impute*

in to or toward; at
inn public lodging house

in sight in view
incite to move to action; to urge on
insight intuitive discernment

in thrall, enthrall
See *enthrall, in thrall*

inane vacant; foolish
insane mentally unstable

inapt not suitable
inept lacking in fitness or aptitude

incidence rate of occurrence or influence
incidents occurrences; happenings

incite, insight, in sight
See *in sight, incite, insight*

indemnify to compensate for damage or loss; to protect against loss
indemnity a payment for damages or losses incurred

independence freedom
independents people not subjected to control by others

indict to charge with an offense
indite to write down; to proclaim

indigenous, endogenous
See *endogenous, indigenous*

indigent poor
indignant angry

indiscreet imprudent
indiscrete not separated into parts

indite, indict
See *indict, indite*

inept, inapt
See *inapt, inept*

inequity injustice; unfairness
iniquity wickedness

infarction process involving dying of tissue
infraction violation

infect to contaminate
infest to overrun in large numbers

infraction, infarction
See *infarction, infraction*

ingenious clever; resourceful
ingenuous showing innocent or child-like simplicity

inhuman lacking pity; savage
inhumane cruel

iniquity, inequity
See *inequity, iniquity*

inn, in
See *in, inn*

innervate, enervate
See *enervate, innervate*

innocence freedom from guilt or sin
innocents those who are innocent

insane, inane
See *inane, insane*

insidious seductive; treacherous
invidious causing discontent or
   envy

insight, in sight, incite
See *in sight, incite, insight*

insoluble undissolvable
insolvable cannot be solved
insolvent bankrupt

instance illustration; example
instants small spaces of time

insure, assure, ensure
See *assure, ensure, insure*

intense existing in an extreme
   degree
intents purposes; meanings

inter, enter
See *enter, inter*

inter- between; among
intra- within

interpret to translate
interrupt to break into

interstate between states
intestate dying without a will
intrastate within a state

intra-, inter-
See *inter-, intra-*

intrastate, interstate, intestate
See *interstate, intestate, intrastate*

invade to encroach upon or
   infringe
inveighed attacked in words;
   assailed

invidious, insidious
See *insidious, invidious*

irascible, erasable
See *erasable, irascible*

irrelevant not relevant or germane
irreverent lacking in proper
   respect

irrupt, erupt
See *erupt, irrupt*

isle, aisle, I'll
See *aisle, I'll, isle*

islet, eyelet
See *eyelet, islet*

its belonging to it
it's it is

J

jam crush; difficult spot; jelly
jamb side of a door or window

jealous envious
zealous ardent

jeans, genes
See *genes, jeans*

jest, gist
See *gist, jest*

jibe, jive, gibe
See *gibe, jibe, jive*

jointer planing tool for joining
boards
jointure act of joining; wife's estate

judicial pertaining to courts of law
judicious wise; discreet

K

kernel, colonel
See *colonel, kernel*

key tool to operate lock; clue;
means of gaining entry
quay wharf

kibbutz collective farm
kibitz to volunteer advice

kill *n.* instance of killing; *v.* to slay
kiln oven

knap to knock; to shape by quick
blows
nap brief, light sleep

knave rogue
nave main part of a church's
interior

knead to press with the hands; to
mold

kneed struck with the knee
need to want; to lack

knew past tense of *know*
new recent; novel

knight medieval gentleman-soldier
night opposite of day

knit to link or cause to grow
together
nit louse or its egg

knob rounded protuberance
nob one in a superior position in
life

knot tying; lump or knob
not negative
naught nothing; zero

knotty full of knots; complex
naughty disobedient

know to be aware of
no not any; negative

knows is aware of
noes plural of *no*
nose organ of smell

kohl, coal, cole
See *coal, cole, kohl*

kraft, craft
See *craft, kraft*

L

laboratory place equipped for scientific experiment
lavatory washbasin; washroom

lacks is without
lacs resinous substances
lax loose

lade to load
laid past tense of *lay*

lain past perfect tense of *lie*
lane narrow road

lam sudden flight
lamb young sheep

lane, lain
See *lain, lane*

laps *n.* plural of *lap; v.* drinks
lapse *n.* slight error; *v* to let slip or pass

later tardier; at a future time
latter of or relating to the second person or group

lath thin narrow strip of wood
lathe type of machine

latter, later
See *later, latter*

lavatory, laboratory
See *laboratory, lavatory*

lax, lacks, lacs
See *lacks, lacs, lax*

lay to put or set down; past tense of *lie*
lei wreath of flowers

lays deposits, as an egg
laze to act or lie lazily

lea grassland
lee side protected from the wind

leach to subject to the action of percolating liquid
leech sucking worm

lead *n.* metal; *v.* to guide
led past tense of *lead*

leaf part of a plant; page of a book
lief gladly

leak *n.* crack or hole that lets something escape *v.* to let out or in accidentally
leek vegetable

lean lacking in fat
lien legal right to a debtor's property

leased rented
least smallest
lest for fear that

led, lead
See *lead, led*

lee, lea
See *lea, lee*

leech, leach
See *leach, leech*

leek, leak
See *leak, leek*

legible, eligible, illegible
See *eligible, illegible, legible*

legislator lawmaker
legislatore body or group of
lawmakers

lei, lay
See *lay, lei*

lemon sour fruit
limen threshold

lends makes a loan
lens optical glass; part of the eye

lessen to shrink or decrease
lesson something learned or
studied

lesser smaller; alternate compara-
tive of *little*
lessor one who grants a lease

lesson, lessen
See *lessen, lesson*

lessor, lesser
See *lesser, lessor*

lest, leased, least
See *leased, least, lest*

levee embankment
levy assessment

liable responsible; subject to
something possible or likely
libel to defame, usually in writing

liar one who tells an untruth
lyre ancient harp-like instrument

libel, liable
See *liable, libel*

lichen type of fungus-like plant
liken to compare

licker one who licks
liqueur sweetened alcoholic
beverage
liquor liquid, especially alcoholic

lie falsehood
lye caustic substance

lief, leaf
See *leaf, lief*

lien, lean
See *lean, lien*

lightening reducing in weight or
quantity
lightning atmospheric electrical
discharge

liken, lichen
See *lichen, liken*

limb arm, leg, or wing; large branch
of a tree
limn to paint or draw

limen, lemon
See *lemon, limen*

limn, limb
See *limb, limn*

linage number of lines of printed or written matter
lineage descent in line from a common progenitor

lineal composed of or arranged in lines; hereditary
linear of, to, or resembling a line; straight

lineament outline, feature, or contour of the body
liniment salve

linear, lineal
See *lineal, linear*

liniment, lineament
See *lineament, liniment*

links connecting structures, as in a chain
lynx wild animal

liqueur, liquor, licker
See *licker, liqueur, liquor*

literal actual; obvious; not figurative
littoral, of, to, or growing on or near a shore

lo expression of wonder
low opposite of *high*

load *n.* burden; *v.* to place in or on
lode ore deposit
lowed mooed

loan something borrowed
lone sole; solitary

loath reluctant
loathe to hate

local characterized by or relating to position in space
locale locality

locks fastenings
lox liquid oxygen; smoked salmon

locus place
locust grasshopper; variety of tree

lode, load, lowed
See *load, lode, lowed*

lone, loan
See *loan, lone*

loop fold of cord or ribbon
loupe small magnifier used by jewelers

loose not tight
lose to experience loss

loot goods stolen or taken by force
lute old stringed instrument

lore knowledge; learning
lower to make low

lose, loose
See *loose, lose*

loupe, loop
See *loop, loupe*

low, lo
See *lo, low*

lowed, lode, load
See *load, lode, lowed*

lower, lore
See *lore, lower*

lox, locks
See *locks, lox*

lumbar of or near loins
lumber timber sawed into convenient sizes

lute, loot
See *loot, lute*

lye, lie
See *lie, lye*

lynx, links
See *links, lynx*

lyre, liar
See *liar, lyre*

M

Macintosh type of computer developed by Apple Computer, Inc.
mackintosh raincoat
McIntosh type of apple; surname

macro *n.* series of keystrokes saved as a unit; *adj* large; prominent
micro very small

macroscopic large enough to be seen by the eye
microscopic invisible or indistinguishable without a microscope

maddening enraging
madding frenzied

made manufactured
maid young girl; servant

magnate person of power or influence
magnet something that attracts

magnificent grand; sumptuous
munificent lavish; liberal

maid, made
See *made, maid*

mail postal matter
male masculine

main principal
Maine New England state
mane long hair growing around neck

maize corn
maze confusing, intricate network of passages

male, mail
See *mail, male*

man's possessive of *man*
manse residence of a minister; large house

mandrel metal bar, axle, or spindle
mandrill large fierce baboon

mane, main, Maine
See *main, Maine, mane*

manner way of acting
manor mansion

manse, man's
See *man's, manse*

mantel shelf above a fireplace
mantle cloak

mare female horse
mayor city's chief executive

marital of or relating to marriage
martial warlike
marshal officer in charge of
prisoners

marry to wed
merry full of gaiety or high spirits

marshal, marital, martial
See *marital, marshal, martial*

marten small animal
martin European sparrow

martial, marital, marshal
See *marital, marshal, martial*

martin, marten
See *marten, martin*

mask covering for the face or part
of the face
masque masked ball; form of
dramatic entertainment

mass aggregate; religious service
mess confused jumble; meal

massed assembled into a mass
mast part of a ship's rigging

mat rug for wiping shoes
matte crude mixture of sulfides;
having a dull finish

material substance
materiel equipment; arms

matte, mat
See *mat, matte*

may be could be
maybe possibly; perhaps

mayor, mare
See *mare, mayor*

maze, maize
See *maize, maze*

**McIntosh, Macintosh, mackin-
tosh**
See *Macintosh, mackintosh,
McIntosh*

mean *adj.* malicious; halfway
between extremes; *v.* to intend
mien bearing or appearance

meat animal flesh used as food;
edible part of anything
meet to come face to face with
mete to distribute; to allot fairly

medal stamped piece of metal
given as an award
meddle to interfere

median middle point
medium intermediate in quality,
size, amount, etc.

mediate to be a go-between; to help settle a dispute
meditate to engage in deep thought

medium, median
See *median, medium*

meet, mete, meat
See *meat, meet, mete*

meretricious tawdrily and falsely attractive
meritorious deserving of honor or award

merry, marry
See *marry, merry*

mess, mass
See *mass, mess*

metal substance
mettle quality of character or temperament

mete, meat, meet
See *meat, meet, mete*

mettle, metal
See *metal, mettle*

mews back street; alley; sounds of a cat
muse source of inspiration

micro, macro
See *macro, micro*

microscopic, macroscopic
See *macroscopic, microscopic*

mien, mean
See *mean, mien*

might power; energy; strength
mite tiny arachnid; very little bit; small coin

millenary group of a thousand
millinery women's apparel for the head

mince small chopped bits
mints confections flavored with mint

mind brain
mined dig from the earth

miner one who mines
minor underage person

minks certain fur-bearing animals
minx pert girl

minor, miner
See *miner, minor*

mints, mince
See *mince, mints*

minx, minks
See *minks, minx*

missal prayer book
missile object or weapon that is thrown or projected

missed failed to hit or reach
mist fine rain; film

missile, missal
See *missal, missile*

mite, might
See *might, mite*

moan low sound of pain; lament
mown past tense of *mow*

moat wide trench usually filled
with water
mote small particle; speck

modal pertaining to mode
model serving as a pattern

mode manner; style
mowed past tense of *mow*

model, modal
See *modal, model*

monetary relating to money or
currency
monitory admonishing; warning

moniker nickname
monitor something or someone
who warns or cautions

monitory, monetary
See *monetary, monitory*

mood one's emotional state
mooed lowed

moors expanses of open grassland
Moors conquerors of Spain in the
eighth century
mores moral attitudes; customs

moose ruminant animal
mousse chilled dessert

moot open to question; debatable;
no need to resolve
mute characterized by absence of
speech or sound

moral ethical; lesson
morale spirit

morality moral conduct; virtue
mortality quality or state of being
mortal

mores, moors, Moors
See *moors, Moors, mores*

morning before noon
mourning act of grieving

mortality, morality
See *morality, mortality*

mote, moat
See *moat, mote*

motif dominant idea or theme
motive something that causes a
person to act

mourning, morning
See *morning, mourning*

mousse, moose
See *moose, mousse*

mowed, mode
See *mode, mowed*

mown, moan
See *moan, mown*

mucous of a viscous substance
mucus viscous substance

munificent, magnificent
See *magnificent munificent*

muscat grape
musket heavy shoulder gun

muscle body tissue; brawn; power
mussel bivalve mollusk
muzzle animal jaws; cover for an
   animal's mouth; discharging end
   of a firearm

muse, mews
See *mews, muse*

musket, muscat
See *muscat, musket*

mussed made untidy
must to be obliged to

mussel, muscle, muzzle
See *muscle, mussel, muzzle*

must, mussed
See *mussed, must*

mustard condiment
mustered formally enrolled;
   caused to gather

mute, moot
See *moot, mute*

mutual having the same feelings
   one for the other
mutuel short for *pari-mutuel;*
   betting pool

muzzle, mussel, muscle
See *muscle, mussel, muzzle*

N

nap, knap
See *knap, nap*

naught, knot, not
See *knot, naught, not*

naughty, knotty
See *knotty, naughty*

naval of the navy
navel umbilicus (belly button)

nave, knave
See *knave, nave*

navel, naval
See *naval, navel*

nay negative reply or vote
neigh cry of a horse
nee used to identify a woman by
   her maiden name

need, knead, kneed
See *knead, kneed, need*

neigh, nay, nee
See *nay, nee, neigh*

neither not either
nether situated down or below

new, knew
See *knew, new*

night, knight
See *knight, night*

nit, knit
See *knit, nit*

no, know
See *know, no*

nob, knob
See *knob, nob*

noes, knows, nose
See *knows, noes, nose*

none not any; nothing
nun woman in a religious order

nose, knows, noes
See *knows, noes, nose*

not, knot, naught
See *knot, naught, not*

nun, none
See *none, nun*

oar long pole for propelling a boat
or conjunction suggesting an
   alternative
ore mineral containing valuable
   metal

ode lyric poem
owed obligated to

offal, awful
See *awful, offal*

oh exclamation of surprise
owe to be obligated

oleo margarine
olio miscellaneous mixture;
   hodgepodge

omission, emission
See *emission, omission*

once one time and no more;
   formerly
wants desires; needs

one first in a series; single item
won past tense of *win*

opposite, apposite
See *apposite, opposite*

or, oar, ore
See *oar, or, ore*

oracle, auricle
See *auricle, oracle*

oral, aural
See *aural, oral*

order arrangement
ordure excrement

ordinance law
ordnance military supplies,
   especially weapons and
   ammunition

ordure, order
See *order, ordure*

ore, oar, or
See *oar, or, ore*

oscillate to swing back and forth
   like a pendulum
osculate to kiss

ought, aught
See *aught, ought*

ours, hours
See *hours, ours*

overdo to do too much; to exhaust; to exaggerate
overdue delayed beyond set time

overseas beyond or across the sea
oversees surveys; supervises

owe, oh
See *oh, owe*

owed, ode
See *ode, owed*

P

paced covered at a walk; measured by pacing
paste adhesive material; kind of dough

packed crammed; past tense of *pack*
pact agreement

paean song of joy
peon member of the landless laboring class

pail bucket
pale deficient in color

pain discomfort
pane framed sheet of glass

pair twosome
pare to trim; to peel
pear fruit

palate roof of mouth; taste
palette artist's board
pallet crude bed; platform

pale, pail
See *pail, pale*

palette, pallet, palate
See *palate, palette, pallet*

palpate to examine by touch
palpitate to beat rapidly; to throb

paltry inferior; trivial
poultry domestic fowls

pane, pain
See *pain, pane*

parameter arbitrary constant whose value characterizes a member of a system
perimeter boundary; outer limits

parcel package; unit
partial biased; of or relating to a part, not the whole

pare, pair, pear
See *pair, pare, pear*

parish ecclesiastical unit
perish to die

parlay to increase or transform into something of greater value
parley to confer; to discuss terms with an enemy

parol word of mouth
parole conditional release of a
prisoner

parson clergyman
person individual human being

partial, parcel
See *parcel, partial*

partition division; something that
divides
petition earnest request; entreaty

passed past tense of *pass*
past former time

paste, paced
See *paced, paste*

patience ability to bear pains,
trials, or delays without complaint
patients individuals awaiting or
under medical care

pause temporary stop
paws feet of animals

peace calmness
piece part

peak summit; promontory
peek brief look; glance
pique transient feeling of wounded
vanity

peal to ring
peel to strip off an outer layer

pear, pare, pair
See *pair, pare, pear*

pearl smooth rounded mass found
in certain mollusks
purl to knit with a particular stitch

pedal foot lever
peddle to sell
petal portion of a flower

peek, peak, pique
See *peak, peek, pique*

peel, peal
See *peal, peel*

peer one who is of equal standing
with another
pier supporting structure; structure
extending into navigable water

pencil writing instrument
pensile suspended

pendant something suspended, as
an ornament on a necklace
pendent supported from above;
suspended

pensile, pencil
See *pencil, pensile*

peon, paean
See *paean, peon*

per by means of; through
purr low vibratory murmur typical
of a contented cat

perceptive having keen insight
preceptive instructive

peremptory admitting of no contradiction
preemptory pertaining to prior rights

perfect without any flaws
prefect administrative official

perform to do; to put into effect; to act
preform to shape beforehand

perimeter, parameter
See *parameter, perimeter*

perish, parish
See *parish, perish*

perpetrate to bring about; to commit
perpetuate to cause to last indefinitely

persecute to hound
prosecute to institute legal action against

person, parson
See *parson, person*

personal relating to a person; private
personnel makeup of an office force

personality complex of characteristics that distinguishes an individual
personalty personal property

personnel, personal
See *personal, personnel*

perspective vision; view
prospective future

peruse to read; to look over
pursue to chase; to follow

petal, pedal, peddle
See *pedal, peddle, petal*

petition, partition
See *partition, petition*

petite small; dainty
petty insignificant

phalanges, flanges
See *flanges, phalanges*

phase, faze
See *faze, phase*

philter, filter
See *filter, philter*

phlox, flocks
See *flocks, phlox*

phrase, frays
See *frays, phrase*

physic medicine, especially a purgative
physique bodily makeup
psychic of or relating to the soul, spirit, or mind

physical, fiscal
See *fiscal, physical*

pi mathematical ratio; term used in printing
pie type of dessert

piazza open public square
pizza baked dough covered with various ingredients

picaresque of or relating to rogues or rascals
picturesque resembling a picture; vivid or graphic

picture *n.* drawing or painting; mental image; *v* to imagine
pitcher container for liquids; baseball player who throws the ball to the batter

picturesque, picaresque
See *picaresque, picturesque*

pidgin simplified speech
pigeon bird

pie, pi
See *pi, pie*

piece, peace
See *peace, piece*

pier, peer
See *peer, pier*

pigeon, pidgin
See *pidgin, pigeon*

pipette slender pipe or tube for taking up small amounts of liquid
pipit bird with a slender bill and a streaked breast

pique, peak, peek
See *peak, peek, pique*

pistil ovule-bearing organ of a seed plant
pistol short firearm

pitcher, picture
See *picture, pitcher*

pixie fairy; elf
pyxie creeping evergreen plant with white, star-shaped flowers

pizza, piazza
See *piazza, pizza*

place physical environment
plaice any of various flat-fishes
plays actions during a game; stage presentations

plain simple
plane *n.* airplane; *v.* to smooth

plaintiff one who commences legal action
plaintive melancholy

plait braid, specifically a pigtail
plat map or plan
plate dish; smooth flat thin piece of material

plane, plain
See *plain, plane*

plantar of or relating to the sole of the foot
planter one that cultivates plants; container for ornamental plants

plat, plate, plait
See *plait, plat, plate*

plays, place, plaice
See *place, plaice, plays*

pleas entreaties; petitions
please to give pleasure

plum fruit
plumb straight down or up

pole rod
Pole native of Poland
poll casting or recording of votes

pooch slang for a dog
putsch sudden political uprising

poor indigent
pore *n.* small opening in the skin;
v. to gaze at intently
pour to cause to flow in a stream

poplar kind of tree
popular widely liked

populace common people
populous densely populated

popular, poplar
See *poplar, popular*

populous, populace
See *populace, populous*

pore, poor, pour
See *poor, pore, pour*

portent omen
potent powerful; strong

portion share of something; part
potion drink; dose

potent, portent
See *potent, portent*

potion, portion
See *portion, potion*

poultry, paltry
See *paltry, poultry*

pour, poor, pore
See *poor, pore, pour*

practicable feasible
practical suited to actual conditions

praise expression of approval
prays entreats
preys *n.* plural of *prey; v.* seizes
and devours; commits violence

precede to go before
proceed to continue

precedence fact of preceding in
time; priority
precedents acts or decisions that
may serve as examples for later
ones

preceding going before in time or
place
proceeding legal action;
transaction

preceptive, perceptive
See *perceptive, preceptive*

preemptory, peremptory
See *peremptory, preemptory*

prefect, perfect
See *perfect, prefect*

preform, perform
See *perform, preform*

premise something taken for granted
promise pledge

preposition part of speech; connecting word
proposition proposal; offer

prescribe to recommend
proscribe to prohibit

presence fact or condition of being present
presents gifts

presentiment foreboding
presentment act of presenting

presents, presence
See *presence, presents*

pretest preliminary test
pretext excuse; action that cloaks the real intention

preys, praise, prays
See *praise, prays, preys*

pride justifiable self-respect; group of lions
pried past tense of *pry*

pries makes a nosy inquiry; moves or pulls apart with a pry or lever
prize *n.* something striven for in competition; *v.* to esteem

prince male member of a royal family
prints copies

princes king's sons
princess king's daughter

principal chief; head person; capital sum
principle rule

prints, prince
See *prince, prints*

prize, pries
See *pries, prize*

proceed, precede
See *precede, proceed*

proceeding, preceding
See *preceding, proceeding*

profit gain
prophet one who predicts the future

promise, premise
See *premise, promise*

prophecy prediction
prophesy to predict

prophet, profit
See *profit, prophet*

propose to suggest; to set forth
purpose *n.* something one intends to do; *v.* to intend

proposition, preposition
See *preposition, proposition*

pros professionals; affirmative side
prose ordinary language of speaking and writing

proscribe, prescribe
See *prescribe, proscribe*

prose, pros
See *pros, prose*

prosecute, persecute
See *persecute, prosecute*

prospective, perspective
See *perspective, prospective*

prostate male gland
prostrate lying flat

protean readily assuming different shapes or roles; variable; diversified
protein nitrogenous organic compound

proximate, approximate
See *approximate, proximate*

psychic, physic, physique
See *physic, physique, psychic*

purl, pearl
See *pearl, purl*

purlin horizontal member in a roof supporting the rafters
purloin to appropriate wrongly; to steal

purpose, propose
See *propose, purpose*

purr, per
See *per, purr*

pursue, peruse
See *peruse, pursue*

pus viscous fluid formed in infected tissue
puss affectionate term for a cat

putsch, pooch
See *pooch, putsch*

pyxie, pixie
See *pixie, pyxie*

qualify to modify; to exhibit a required degree of ability
quantify to determine the quantity of

qualitative of or relating to quality or kind
quantitative of, relating to, or expressible in terms of quantity

quantify, qualify
See *qualify, quantify*

quantitative, qualitative
See *qualitative, quantitative*

quarts units of capacity
quartz mineral

quay, key
See *key, quay*

queue, cue
See *cue, queue*

quire, choir
See *choir, quire*

quitter person who quits
quittor foot disease of horses

quoin, coin
See *coin, quoin*

R

rabbet channel or groove
rabbit small long-eared mammal
rarebit Welsh rabbit; popular
    British dish

rack grating; framework; antlers;
    instrument of torture
wrack to ruin utterly; to destroy; to
    torture

racket clamor
racquet lightweight implement
    used in various games

radical extreme
radicle root

radish vegetable
reddish somewhat red

raid hostile or predatory incursion
rayed shone in or on; radiated

rail *n.* a bar of wood or metal; *v.* to
    speak bitterly; *adj.* referring to
    the railroad
rale abnormal sound accompany-
    ing normal sounds of breathing

rain to fall, as water; to pour down
rein to check or stop
reign to rule

raise to elevate; to build
rays beams of light, etc..
raze to destroy to the ground

raiser one that raises
razor shaving instrument

rale, rail
See *rail, rale*

rancor bitter ill will; enmity
ranker more luxuriant in growth;
    more offensive or shocking

rap sharp blow or knock
wrap *n.* outer garment; *v.* to cover
    by winding or folding; to bundle
    up

rapped tapped or knocked
rapt enraptured; absorbed
wrapped enveloped

rarebit, rabbet, rabbit
See *rabbet, rabbit, rarebit*

rational having reason or under-
    standing
rationale underlying reason; basis

ravage to wreak havoc on; to
  devastate
ravish to seize and take away by
  violence; to rape; to plunder

ray beam of light
re with regard to

rayed, raid
See *raid, rayed*

rays, raise, raze
See *raise, rays, raze*

razor, raiser
See *raiser, razor*

re, ray
See *ray, re*

read past tense of *read*
red color

read to peruse
reed tall grass

real actual; genuine
reel revolving device on which
  something flexible is wound

reality quality or state of being real
realty real estate

rebait to bait again
rebate to return part of a payment

rebound to spring back; to recoil
redound to have an effect or
  consequence; to accrue

recede to withdraw or ebb
reseed to seed again

receipt acknowledgment
reseat to seat again

recent done not long ago
resent to feel injured or angry at

reck to reckon
wreck to ruin or damage

red, read
See *read, red*

reddish, radish
See *radish, reddish*

redound, rebound
See *rebound, redound*

reed, read
See *read, reed*

reek to give off a strong, unpleas-
  ant odor
wreak to inflict

reel, real
See *real, reel*

reference something that refers
referents those who refer or are
  referred to

reflects throws back; considers
reflex automatic and often inborn
  response

regime regular pattern; government
regimen systematic plan
regiment military unit

register written record; roster
registrar official recorder or
keeper of records; admitting
officer

regretfully sorrowfully
regrettable unfortunate

reign, rain, rein
See *rain, reign, rein*

relaid laid again
relayed passed along, as a mes-
sage, by relays

relative regarded in relation to
something else; kinsman
relevant pertinent

relic memento; souvenir
relict widow; something left
behind

renegade deserter from a cause
renege to back out; to fail to follow
up or fulfill

repeal to do away with; to annul
repel to force back; to cause
disgust

reseat, receipt
See *receipt, reseat*

reseed, recede
See *recede, reseed*

resent, recent
See *recent, resent*

residence domicile
residency official place of residence; period of advanced
medical training
residents those who reside in a
place

respectably decently
respectfully showing respect or
deference
respectively in the order given

rest to repose
wrest to gain by force or violence

retch to try to vomit
wretch miserable and unhappy
person; vile person

reverend a member of the clergy
reverent expressing reverence;
worshipful

review inspection, especially
military; critical examination
revue theatrical production
consisting of short skits, dances,
etc.

rheumy having a watery discharge
from the mucous membranes
roomy spacious

rhyme poetry
rime frost

ridged formed into a ridge
rigid still; unyielding

rigger one that rigs; type of ship
rigor severity; strictness; austerity

right correct; opposite of left
rite ceremony
wright workman
write to form characters on a
surface as with a pen

rigid, ridged
See *ridged, rigid*

rigor, rigger
See *rigger, rigor*

rime, rhyme
See *rhyme, rime*

ring to sound; to reverberate; to
encircle
wring to squeeze or twist, especially so as to make dry

risky dangerous
risqué off-color

rite, right, wright, write
See *right, rite, wright, write*

ritz pretentious display
writs legal instruments

road path; highway
rode past tense of *ride*
rowed propelled a small boat

roes deer; fish eggs
rose *n.* flower; *v.* ascended
rows *n.* objects arranged in lines; *v.*
propels a small boat

role part
roll *n.* bread; *v.* to turn

rood cross or crucifix
rude unmannerly; crude; vulgar
rued regretted

roomer one who rents a room
rumor report; hearsay; gossip

roomy, rheumy
See *rheumy, roomy*

root underground portion of a
plant; origin or source
rout disastrous defeat
route traveled way; channel

rose, roes, rows
See *roes, rose, rows*

rot decay
wrought worked

rote repetition by memory
wrote past tense of *write*

rough coarse; harsh; uneven
ruff *n.* fringe, as of feathers,
around the neck; *v.* to trump a
trick at bridge

rout, route, root
See *root, rout, route*

roux cooked mixture of melted
butter and flour used for sauces
rue *n.* strong-scented shrub; *v.* to
feel remorse

rowed, road, rode
See *road, rode, rowed*

rows, roes, rose
See *roes, rose, rows*

rude, rood, rued
See *rood, rude, rued*

rue, roux
See *roux, rue*

rued, rood, rude
See *rood, rude, rued*

ruff, rough
See *rough, ruff*

rumor, roomer
See *roomer, rumor*

rung *n.* step on a ladder; *v.* past tense of *ring*
wrung past tense of *wring*

rye grain; whiskey
wry bent or twisted

sacks bags
sacs pouches
sax saxophone

sail *n.* canvas by which wind propels a ship; *v.* propelling a ship by wind
sale act of selling

sallow sickly yellow color
shallow having little depth

salon elegant apartment or living room; stylish shop
saloon tavern

salvage *n.* property saved from destruction; *v.* to save from disaster
selvage edge of fabric that is finished to prevent raveling

sane mentally sound
seine net for catching fish

sassy impudent
saucy bold and impudent; flippant

satire literary work where irony or derision exposes folly or wickedness
satyr woodland deity; lecherous man

saucy, sassy
See *sassy, saucy*

saver one who saves
savior one who saves others from death or destruction
savor *n.* taste or smell of something; *v.* to relish or enjoy

sax, sacs, sacks
See *sacks, sacs, sax*

scam scandal
scan to examine closely

scene subdivision of a play
seen form of *see*

scents, cents, sense
See *cents, scents, sense*

scion descendant
sign signal
sine trigonometric function of an
    angle
syne since

Scotch *n.* whiskey; *adj.* pertaining
    to Scotland
Scots natives of Scotland

scrimp to be frugal
skimp to give insufficient or barely
    sufficient attention or effort to or
    funds for

scrip brief note; paper money
script handwriting; manuscript of
    text for film, radio, etc.

scull oar used at the stern of a boat;
    racing shell
skull framework of the head

sculptor artist who produces
    sculpture
sculpture three-dimensional work
    of art

sea body of water
see *n.* seat of church authority; *v.*
    to perceive with the eye

sealing, ceiling
See *ceiling, sealing*

seam joining of two pieces
seem to appear

sear to cause withering or drying
seer one that sees; prophet
sere withered (poetic)

seas, cease, sees, seize
See *cease, seas, sees, seize*

seasonable appropriate to the
    season; timely
seasonal depending on the season

secret something hidden or
    unexplained
secrete to conceal

sects factions
sex gender; sexual intercourse

see, sea
See *sea, see*

seed, cede
See *cede, seed*

seem, seam
See *seam, seem*

seen, scene
See *scene, seen*

seer, sear, sere
See *sear, seer, sere*

sees, cease, seas, seize
See *cease, seas, sees, seize*

seine, sane
See *sane, seine*

seize, cease, seas, sees
See *cease, seas, sees, seize*

sell, cell
See *cell, sell*

seller, cellar
See *cellar, seller*

selvage, salvage
See *salvage, selvage*

sense, cents, scents
See *cents, scents, sense*

senses, census
See *census, senses*

sensor, censer, censor, censure
See *censer, censor, censure, sensor*

sequence succession of related
   elements
sequins spangles

sere, sear, seer
See *sear, seer, sere*

serf member of a servile feudal
   class
surf swell of the sea that breaks on
   the shore

serge durable twilled fabric
surge swelling, rolling, or sweeping
   forward, like ocean waves

serial, cereal
See *cereal, serial*

serious, serous, cirrous, cirrus
See *cirrous, cirrus, serious, serous*

session, cession
See *cession, session*

sew to unite or fasten by stitches
so thus
sow to plant seed, especially by
   scattering

sewage refuse or waste matter
   carried by sewers
sewerage sewage; disposal of
   sewage by sewers

sewer conduit for waste matter
suer one who sues

sewerage, sewage
See *sewage, sewerage*

sex, sects
See *sects, sex*

shake to vibrate
sheik Arab chief

shallow, sallow
See *sallow, shallow*

sham hoax
shame disgrace; ignominy

sheaf ears of grain, etc., bound
   together; collection of papers,
   etc., held or bound together
sheath cover or case
sheet piece of paper; broad piece
   of cloth

shear to clip
sheer transparent; utter

sheath, sheaf, sheet
See *sheaf, sheath, sheet*

sheer, shear
See *shear, sheer*

sheet, sheath, sheaf
See *sheaf, sheath, sheet*

sheik, chic
See *chic, sheik*

sheik, shake
See *shake, sheik*

shoe *n.* footwear; *v.* to provide
footwear
shoo to scare or drive away

shone past tense of *shine*
shown form of *show*

shoo, shoe
See *shoe, shoo*

shoot, chute
See *chute, shoot*

shortened curtailed
shorthand abbreviated

shown, shone
See *shone, shown*

shudder to tremble or quiver
shutter movable cover or screen
for a window

sic used to show word or phrase
was intentional; to chase or
attack
sick ill

side lateral
sighed uttered a sigh

sighs utters a sigh
size physical magnitude, extent, or
bulk

sight, cite, site
See *cite, sight, site*

sign, scion, sine, syne
See *scion, sign, sine, syne*

silicon nonmetallic element
silicone polymeric silicon compound

simulate to copy or represent
stimulate to excite to activity or
growth; to arouse

sine, scion, sign, syne
See *scion, sign, sine, syne*

sinews tendons
sinuous wavy or serpentine;
intricate

sink to go to the bottom; to
submerge
sync to synchronize

sinuous, sinews
See *sinews, sinuous*

site, sight, cite
See *cite, sight, site*

size, sighs
See *sighs, size*

skimp, scrimp
See *scrimp, skimp*

skull, scull
See *scull, skull*

slay to kill
sleigh sled

sleight strategem; dexterity
slight *v.* to neglect; *adj.* slim; frail; meager

sloe fruit of the blackthorn
slough bog
slow sluggish; dull

smooth to make things more agreeable; to make easier
soothe to calm

so, sew, sow
See *sew, so, sow*

soak to make thoroughly wet; to charge too much
soke right to hold court and dispense justice within a territory

soar to fly aloft or about; to rise to heights; to glide
sore painful

soared rose
sword weapon with a long blade

soiree party or gathering in the evening
sorry full of sorrow

soke, soak
See *soak, soke*

sold past tense of *sell*
soled put soles on shoes

sole undersurface of foot or footwear; type of fish
soul spirit

soled, sold
See *sold, soled*

some indeterminate quantity
sum total

son male child
sun celestial body around which a planet revolves

soothe, smooth
See *smooth, soothe*

sore, soar
See *soar, sore*

sorry, soiree
See *soiree, sorry*

soul, sole
See *sole, soul*

sow, sew
See *sew, sow*

spacious roomy
specious having a false look of truth or genuineness

spade garden tool; card suit
spayed removed the ovaries of

specie money in coin
species class; genus; kind

specious, spacious
See *spacious, specious*

staff rod; personnel
staph staphylococcus infection

staid sedate; sober
stayed past tense of *stay*

stair one of a series of steps
stare fixed look

stake pointed piece of wood
steak slice of meat

stalactite hanging calcium deposit
stalagmite upright calcium deposit

staph, staff
See *staff, staph*

stare, stair
See *stair, stare*

stationary fixed
stationery paper supplies

statue sculpture
stature natural height; quality or
    status
statute law or rule

stayed, staid
See *staid, stayed*

steak, stake
See *stake, steak*

steal to rob
steel *n.* metal; *v.* to make resolute;
    to harden

step ladder rung; manner of
    walking
steppe vast, usually treeless, plain

stile series of steps for passing
    over a fence or wall
style fashion

stimulate, simulate
See *simulate, stimulate*

stop, estop
See *estop, stop*

straight direct; uninterrupted;
    upright
strait *n.* isthmus; *adj.* narrow or
    constricted

straighten to make straight
straiten to make narrow; to
    subject to deprivation

strait, straight
See *straight, strait*

straiten, straighten
See *straighten, straiten*

stricture narrowing or restriction
structure action of building;
    building itself

striped having stripes or streaks
stripped past tense of *strip*

structure, stricture
See *stricture, structure*

style, stile
See *stile, style*

succor relief; help
sucker one that sucks; cheated
    person; hard candy on a stick

suede leather with a napped
    surface
swayed past tense of *sway*

suer, sewer
See *sewer, suer*

suit set of garments
suite set, as a group of rooms
sweet confection; dessert

sum, some
See *some, sum*

summary *n.* synopsis or conclusion; *adj.* quickly executed
summery of, resembling, or fit for summer

summoned convoked; ordered to appear
summonsed summoned by means of a summons

sun, son
See *son, sun*

super outstanding; exceptionally fine
supra above; earlier in this writing

surely certainly
surly churlish; sullen

surf, serf
See *serf, surf*

surge, serge
See *serge, surge*

surly churlish; sullen
surely certainly

surplice ecclesiastical vestment
surplus excess

swatch sample piece
swath sweep of a scythe; long broad strip or belt
swathe *n.* bandage; *v.* to bind or wrap; to bandage

swayed, suede
See *suede, swayed*

sweet, suit, suite
See *suit, suite, sweet*

sword, soared
See *soared, sword*

symbol, cymbal
See *cymbal, symbol*

sync, sink
See *sink, sync*

syne, scion, sign, sine
See *scion, sign, sine, syne*

T

tacked past tense of *tack*
tact diplomacy

tacks attaches with small nails; brings a vessel into the wind
tax *n.* charge levied by authority for public purposes; *v.* to levy a tax on; to make demands on

tact, tacked
See *tacked, tact*

tail rear appendage
tale story

talents abilities
talons claws

talesman member of a jury pool
talisman charm or fetish

talons, talents
See *talents, talons*

taped past tense of *tape*
tapped past tense of *tap*

taper slender candle
tapir animal related to horse and
  rhinoceros

tapped, taped
See *taped, tapped*

tare seed; deduction of container
  weight from gross weight
tear rip or laceration

taught past tense of *teach*
taut tightly drawn; tense

tax, tacks
See *tacks, tax*

tea beverage
tee mound or peg on which a golf
  ball is placed

team to yoke or join in a team
teem to abound; to become filled to
  overflowing

tear, tare
See *tare, tear*

tear saline drop emanating from
  the eye
tier row, rank, or layer of articles

teas late-afternoon receptions
tease to annoy or harass
tees mounds or pegs for golf balls

tee, tea
See *tea, tee*

teem, team
See *team, teem*

tees, teas, tease
See *teas, tease, tees*

tenace bridge term
tennis popular game

tenant lessee; occupant
tenet principle, belief, or doctrine
  held to be true

tenner ten-dollar bill
tenor highest natural male singing
  voice; general sense
tenure act of holding

tennis, tenace
See *tenace, tennis*

tenor, tenner, tenure
See *tenner, tenor, tenure*

tense stretched tight; stiff and
  unrelaxed
tents collapsible canvas shelters

tenure, tenor, tenner
See *tenner, tenor, tenure*

tern type of seagull
turn rotation

Thai native of Thailand
tie bond

than compared to
then at that time

the one designated
thee you

their belonging to them
there at that place
they're contraction for *they are*

theirs belonging to them
there's contraction for *there is*

then, than
See *than, then*

there, their, they're
See *their, there, they're*

therefor for or in return for that
therefore for that reason; conse-
quently

there's, theirs
See *theirs, there's*

they're, their, there
See *their, there, they're*

thorough painstaking; exhaustive
through extending from one
surface to another; finished
threw tossed

thrash to beat soundly
thresh to separate seed at harvest

threw, thorough, through
See *thorough, threw, through*

throes pangs; spasms
throws tosses

throne chair of state for a monarch
thrown tossed

through, thorough, threw
See *thorough, threw, through*

thrown, throne
See *throne, thrown*

throws, throes
See *throes, throws*

thyme garden herb
time duration

tic muscular twitching
tick light rhythmic tap or beat;
blood-sucking mite

tide alternate rising and falling of
the ocean
tied past tense of *tie*

tie, Thai
See *Thai, tie*

tied, tide
See *tide, tied*

tier, tear
See *tear, tier*

timber growing trees or their wood
timbre quality given to a sound by
its overtones

time, thyme
See *thyme, time*

tinny containing tin; bright but
cheap; unmusical sound
tiny very small

to toward
too also; extremely or excessively
two number

toad tailless leaping amphibian
toed having toes; on a slant
towed past tense of *tow*

toe appendage on the foot
tow to draw or pull along behind

toed, toad, towed
See *toad, toed, towed*

toke puff of a cigarette
toque small hat

told past tense of *tell*
tolled rang a bell

ton unit of weight
tun large cask, especially for wine

tonnage, dunnage
See *dunnage, tonnage*

too, to, two
See *to, too, two*

topography geographical configuration
typography style of typeset matter

toque, toke
See *toke, toque*

tortious implying or involving a tort
tortoise turtle
tortuous winding; circuitous; tricky or crooked
torturous causing torture; cruelly painful

tow, toe
See *toe, tow*

towed, toad, toed
See *toad, toed, towed*

tracked past tense of *track*
tract parcel of land; religious or political pamphlet

trail path
trial judicial proceedings

transverse lying or being across
traverse to pass through; to oppose

tray open receptacle with a flat bottom for carrying or displaying articles
trey in cards, the three-spot

treaties agreements
treatise discourse

trey, tray
See *tray, trey*

trial, trail
See *trail, trial*

troop group of soldiers, etc.
troupe group of theatrical performers

trooper soldier or police officer
trouper actor; dependable person

troupe, troop
See *troop, troupe*

trouper, trooper
See *trooper, trouper*

trussed tightly secured; bound
trust faith; confidence

trustee one to whom something is
    entrusted
trusty convict considered
    trustworthy and allowed special
    privileges

tucks folds stitched into cloth
tux tuxedo

tun, ton
See *ton, tun*

turban headdress
turbine rotary engine

turbid obscure; muddy
turgid swollen; pompous

turbine, turban
See *turban, turbine*

turgid, turbid
See *turbid, turgid*

turn, tern
See *tern, turn*

tux, tucks
See *tucks, tux*

two, to, too
See *to, too, two*

typography, topography
See *topography, typography*

U

undo unfasten; nullify
undue exceeding or violating
    propriety or fitness

unexceptionable beyond reproach
unexceptional commonplace

uninterested, disinterested
See *disinterested, uninterested*

unreal lacking in reality
unreel to unwind from a reel

unwanted not wanted
unwonted rare; unusual

urban of, relating to, or constitut-
    ing a city
urbane suave; sophisticated

urn, earn, erne
See *earn, erne, urn*

V

vacation, vocation, avocation
See *avocation, vacation, vocation*

vain conceited
vane device showing wind direc-
    tion
vein narrow channel; lode; blood
    vessel

vale valley
veil face covering; something that
    obscures

vane, vain, vein
See *vain, vane, vein*

variance dispute; deviation
variants persons or things exhibiting slight differences

vary to change; to deviate
very exceedingly

vassal subordinate; servant
vessel utensil for holding something; boat

vault to leap
vaunt to display one's own worth or attainments; to boast

veil, vale
See *vale, veil*

vein, vain, vane
See *vain, vane, vein*

venal corrupt
venial pardonable

veracious truthful
voracious ravenously hungry

veracity truthfulness
voracity state of being ravenously hungry

vertebra any of the bones or segments forming the spinal column
vertebrae plural of *vertebra* (often pronounced the same)

vertex highest point of something
vortex whirling mass of fluid; something resembling a whirlpool

very, vary
See *vary, very*

vessel, vassal
See *vassal, vessel*

vial small vessel for liquids
vile evil; foul
viol stringed musical instrument

vice moral fault or failing
vise tool with tight-holding jaws

vicious mean; violent; fierce
viscous sticky

vile, vial, viol
See *vial, vile, viol*

viral of, relating to, or caused by a virus
virile manly; masterful; forceful

virtu love of or taste for art objects
virtue honor; uprightness

viscous, vicious
See *vicious, viscous*

vise, vice
See *vice, vise*

vocation, avocation, vacation
See *avocation, vacation, vocation*

voracious, veracious
See *veracious, voracious*

voracity, veracity
See *veracity, voracity*

vortex, vertex
See *vertex, vortex*

voyager one who travels
voyeur one who seeks sexual
gratification by visual means

W

wade to step in or through water
weighed past tense of *weigh*

wail mournful cry
wale rib in fabric; ridge
whale sea mammal

waist narrowed part of the body
between chest and hips
waste rejected material; garbage

wait delay
weight heaviness

waive to relinquish voluntarily
wave *n.* swelling in the sea; *v.* to
motion with the hand

waiver voluntary relinquishment of
a right or privilege
waver *n.* one who waves; *v.* to
vacillate

wale, wail, whale
See *wail, wale, whale*

walk stroll; sidewalk
wok cooking pan

want lack
wont custom
won't contraction of *will not*

wants, once
See *once, wants*

war combat
wore past tense of *wear*

ward to deflect; to guard
warred made war on

ware goods
wear to bear or have on the person
where at, in, or to what place

warn to give notice of danger or
evil
worn *v.* past tense of *wear; adj.*
damaged by use

warrantee person to whom a
warranty is made
warranty written guarantee of a
product

warred, ward
See *ward, warred*

wary cautious
weary tired

waste, waist
See *waist, waste*

watt unit of electrical power
what which thing, event, etc.

wave, waive
See *waive, wave*

waver, waiver
See *waiver, waver*

wax substance secreted by bees
whacks resounding blows

way thoroughfare
weigh to ascertain the heaviness of
whey thin part of milk

we personal pronoun
wee tiny

weak lacking strength
week seven days

weal sound, healthy, or prosperous
     state
we'll contraction of *we will*
wheal welt
wheel circular frame designed to
     turn on an axis

wear, where, ware
See *ware, wear, where*

weary, wary
See *wary, weary*

weather state of atmosphere
whether if
wether castrated sheep

weave to interlace into cloth
we've contraction of *we have*

we'd contraction of *we had, we
     should* or *we would*
weed undesired plant

wee, we
See *we, wee*

weed, we'd
See *we'd, weed*

week, weak
See *weak, week*

weigh, way, whey
See *way, weigh, whey*

weighed, wade
See *wade, weighed*

weight, wait
See *wait, weight*

weir fence placed in a stream to
     catch fish
we're contraction of *we are*

we'll, weal, wheal, wheel
See *weal, we'll, wheal, wheel*

wen benign skin growth
when at a specific time

wench young woman; lewd woman
winch machine for hoisting cable
wrench violent twisting; hand tool

we're, weir
See *weir, we're*

wet to douse or dampen
whet to sharpen; to stimulate

wether, weather, whether
See *weather, wether, whether*

we've, weave
See *weave, we've*

whacks, wax
See *wax, whacks*

whale, wale, wail
See *wale, wail, whale*

what, watt
See *watt, what*

wheal, weal, we'll, wheel
See *weal, we'll, wheal, wheel*

when, wen
See *wen, when*

where, ware, wear
See *ware, wear, where*

whet, wet
See *wet, whet*

whether, weather, wether
See *weather, wether, whether*

whey, way, weigh
See *way, weigh, whey*

which what particular one or ones
witch hag

while period of time, usually short
wile trick or stratagem

whine prolonged high-pitched cry, usually of distress or pain
wine fermented beverage

whinny neigh
whiny characterized by whining

whirl rapid rotating or circling movement
whorl coiled, spiral arrangement of similar parts

whit smallest part or particle imaginable
wit humor

white color
wight strong; brisk; active

whither to which place
wither to dry up

whole, hole
See *hole, whole*

who's contraction of *who is* or *who has*
whose of or relating to whom or which

wholly, holy, holey
See *holey, holy, wholly*

whoop, hoop
See *hoop, whoop*

whore, hoar, hoer
See *hoar, hoer, whore*

whored, hoard, horde
See *hoard, horde, whored*

whorl, whirl
See *whirl, whorl*

whose, who's
See *who's, whose*

why for what cause, reason, or purpose
wye letter *y*

wight, white
See *white, wight*

wile, while
See *while, wile*

wince to shrink or draw back
wins triumphs; succeeds
winze inclined shaft between one
level and another in a mine

winch, wrench, wench
See *wench, winch, wrench*

wind to turn completely or repeatedly about an object
wined served wine

wine, whine
See *whine, wine*

wined, wind
See *wind, wined*

winze, wince, wins
See *wince, wins, winze*

wit, whit
See *whit, wit*

witch, which
See *which, witch*

wither, whither
See *whither, wither*

wok, walk
See *walk, wok*

won't, want, wont
See *want, wont, won't*

won, one
See *one, won*

wood lumber
would past tense of *will*

wore, war
See *war, wore*

workaday prosaic; ordinary
workday pertaining to day on
which work is performed

worn, warn
See *warn, worn*

worst most corrupt, bad, or evil
wurst sausage

would, wood
See *wood, would*

wrack, rack
See *rack, wrack*

wrap, rap
See *rap, wrap*

wrapped, rapped, rapt
See *rapped, rapt, wrapped*

wraith ghost
wrath anger

wreak, reek
See *reek, wreak*

wreath ring of flowers or leaves
twisted together
wreathe to twist; to make into a
wreath; to encircle
writhe to twist and turn; to suffer
mentally; to be very
uncomfortable

wreck, reck
See *reck, wreck*

wrench, wench, winch
See *wench, winch, wrench*

wrest, rest
See *rest, wrest*

wretch, retch
See *retch, wretch*

wright, rite, write, right
See *right, rite, wright, write*

wring, ring
See *ring, wring*

write, rite, right, wright
See *right, rite, wright, write*

writhe, wreath, wreathe
See *wreath, wreathe, writhe*

writs, ritz
See *ritz, writs*

wrote, rote
See *rote, wrote*

wrought, rot
See *rot, wrought*

wrung, rung
See *rung, wrung*

wry, rye
See *rye, wry*

wurst, worst
See *worst, wurst*

wye, why
See *why, wye*

Y

yew, you, ewe
See *ewe, yew, you*

yoke wooden frame for joining
together draft animals
yolk yellow of an egg

yore time long ago
your of or belonging to you; having
to do with you
you're contraction of *you are*

you, ewe, yew
See *ewe, yew, you*

you'll contraction of *you will*
yule Christmas

Z

zealous, jealous
See *jealous, zealous*

Available From
SkillPath Publications

Self-Study Sourcebooks

Climbing the Corporate Ladder: What You Need to Know and Do to Be a Promotable Person *by Barbara Pachter and Marjorie Brody*

Discovering Your Purpose *by Ivy Haley*

Mastering the Art of Communication: Your Keys to Developing a More Effective Personal Style *by Michelle Fairfield Poley*

Organized for Success! 95 Tips for Taking Control of Your Time, Your Space, and Your Life *by Nanci McGraw*

Productivity Power: 250 Great Ideas for Being More Productive *by Jim Temme*

Promoting Yourself: 50 Ways to Increase Your Prestige, Power, and Paycheck *by Marlene Caroselli, Ed.D.*

Risk-Taking: 50 Ways to Turn Risks Into Rewards *by Marlene Caroselli, Ed.D. and David Harris*

The Technical Writer's Guide *by Robert McGraw*

Total Quality Customer Service: How to Make It Your Way of Life *by Jim Temme*

Write It Right! A Guide for Clear and Correct Writing *by Richard Andersen and Helene Hinis*

Spiral Handbooks

The ABC's of Empowered Teams: Building Blocks for Success *by Mark Towers*

Assert Yourself! Developing Power-Packed Communication Skills to Make Your Points Clearly, Confidently, and Persuasively *by Lisa Contini*

Breaking the Ice: How to Improve Your On-the-Spot Communication Skills *by Deborah Shouse*

The Care and Keeping of Customers: A Treasury of Facts, Tips and Proven
Techniques for Keeping Your Customers Coming BACK! *by Roy Lantz*

Dynamic Delegation: A Manager's Guide for Active Empowerment
by Mark Towers

Every Woman's Guide to Career Success *by Denise M. Dudley*

Hiring and Firing: What Every Manager Needs to Know
by Marlene Caroselli, Ed.D. with Laura Wyeth, Ms.Ed.

How to Deal With Difficult People *by Paul Friedman*

Learning to Laugh at Work: The Power of Humor in the Workplace
by Robert McGraw

Making Your Mark: How to Develop a Personal Marketing Plan for Becoming More
Visible and More Appreciated at Work *by Deborah Shouse*

Meetings That Work *by Marlene Caroselli, Ed.D.*

The Mentoring Advantage: How to Help Your Career Soar to New Heights
by Pam Grout

Minding Your Business Manners: Etiquette Tips for Presenting Yourself
Professionally in Every Business Situation *by Marjorie Brody
and Barbara Pachter*

Misspeller's Guide *by Joel and Ruth Schroeder*

NameTags Plus: Games You Can Play When People Don't Know What to Say
by Deborah Shouse

Networking: How to Creatively Tap Your People Resources *by Colleen Clarke*

New & Improved! 25 Ways to Be More Creative and More Effective
by Pam Grout

Power Write! A Practical Guide to Words That Work *by Helene Hinis*

Putting Anger to Work For You! *by Ruth and Joel Schroeder*

Reinventing Your Self: 28 Strategies for Coping With Change *by Mark Towers*

The Supervisor's Guide: The Everyday Guide to Coordinating People and Tasks
by Jerry Brown and Denise Dudley, Ph.D.

Taking Charge: A Personal Guide to Managing Projects and Priorities
by Michal E. Feder

Treasure Hunt: 10 Stepping Stones to a New and More Confident You!
by Pam Grout

A Winning Attitude: How to Develop Your Most Important Asset!
by Michelle Fairfield Poley

For more information, call 1-800-873-7545.